Wingham and Blyth Ontario in Colour Photos, Saving Our History One Photo at a Time

Photography
by Barbara Raué
2015

Series Name:
Cruising Ontario

Book 109: Wingham and Blyth

Cover photo: Wingham Town Hall

Series Name: Cruising Ontario
Saving Our History One Photo at a Time
in colour photos

Other Books by Barbara Raue

Coins of Gold

Arrows, Indians and Love

The Life and Times of Barbara
Volume 1: Inventions That Have Enhanced My Life
Volume 2: Entertainment That I Have Enjoyed
Volume 3: East Coast Trips
Volume 4: Olympics Have Always Intrigued Me
Volume 5: Wonders of the World
Volume 6: Caribbean Cruises We Have Enjoyed
Volume 7: Animals
Volume 8: Storms and Other Major Disasters in My Lifetime
Volume 9: Wars, Terrorist Attacks and Major Disasters

The Cromwell Family Book

Laura Secord Discovered

Daddy Where Are You?

Visit Barbara's website to view all of her books
http://barbararaue.ca

Wingham

In the early 1850s, settlers began moving into the townships in the Queen's Bush north of the Huron Tract. One of these townships, Turnberry, was surveyed by 1853 and a plot for a market town was designated where two branches of the Maitland River met. Among the earliest settlers on the plot was John Cornyn who was operating a hotel here in 1861. A year later a post office named Wingham was established and by 1866 Wingham had become a prominent supply and distributing centre for the agricultural and lumbering area. In the 1870s railway expansion stimulated growth and led to Wingham's incorporation as a village in 1874 with a population of 700. Five years later with a population of 2000, Wingham was incorporated as a town.

Wingham, located in Huron County at the intersection of County Roads 4 & 86, became part of North Huron municipality in 2001 when the former township of East Wawanosh, the village of Blyth, and the town of Wingham were amalgamated.

Blyth

Blyth is located southwest of the town of Wingham on Huron Road 4, and geographically south of the town of Lucknow. The community was founded in 1877 and amalgamated into North Huron in 2001. Many of its buildings still retain a Cape Dutch style of detailing that was popular after the Boer War.

Blyth is the center for the nationally acclaimed theatre, the Blyth Festival which, since its inception in 1975, has premiered 121 Canadian plays. Plays developed at the Blyth Festival have won Governor General's Awards and a number of Chalmers Awards. It plays to audiences of between forty and fifty thousand annually.

Table of Contents

Wingham

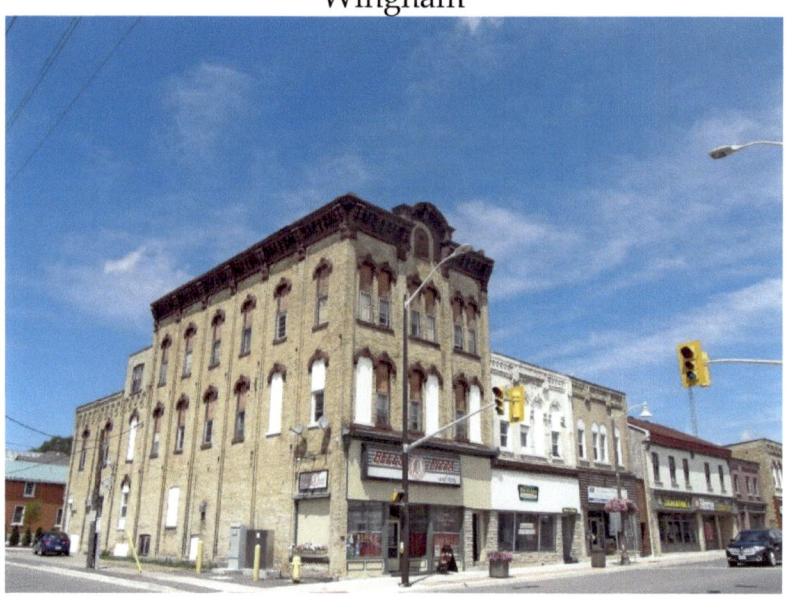

Window hoods with keystones, cornice brackets, pilasters

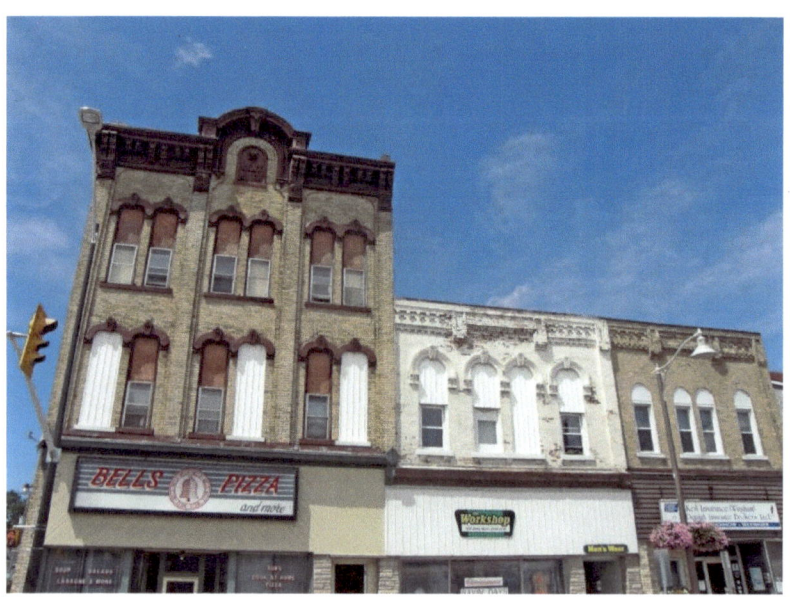

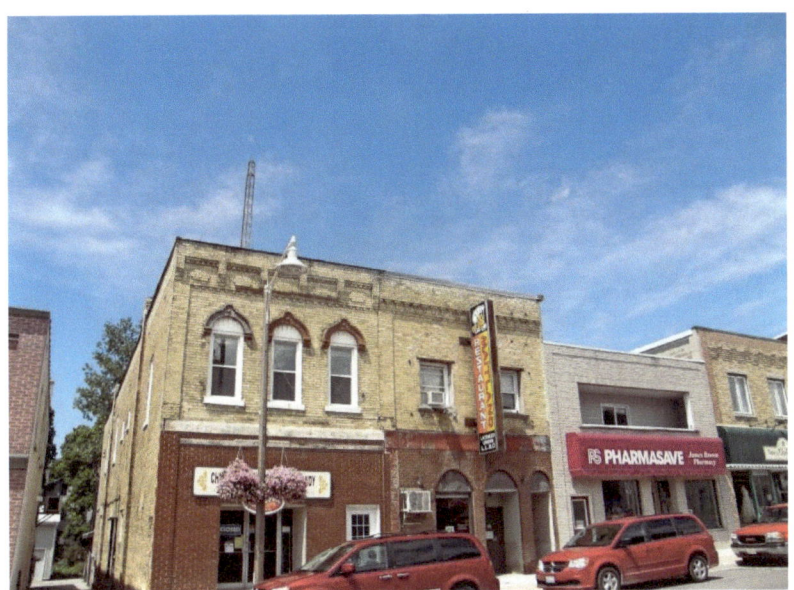
Window hoods, dentil moulding

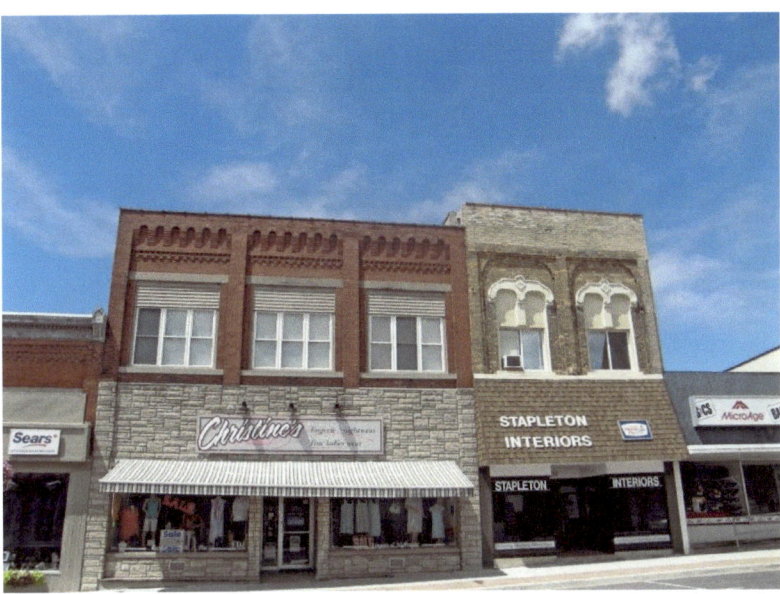
Bevelled and regular dentil moulding, window hoods

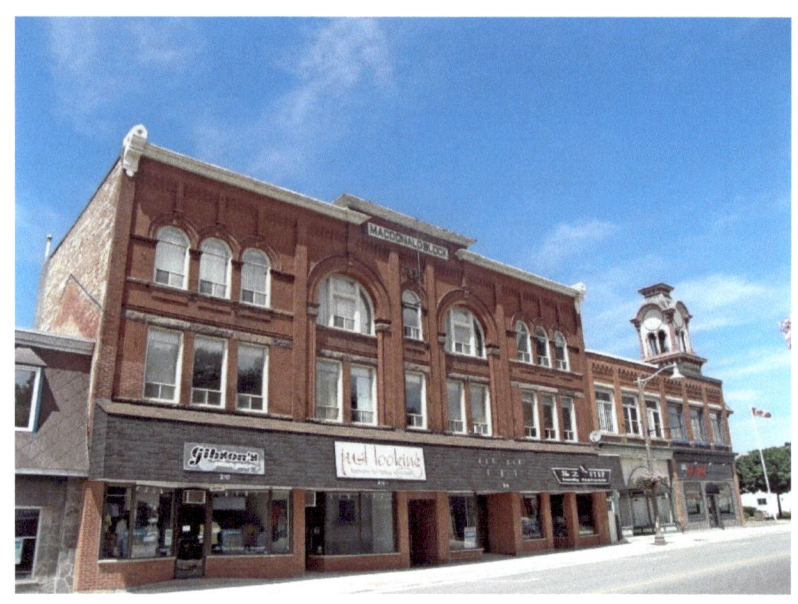

Macdonald Block 1893 – window hoods,
bevelled dentil moulding

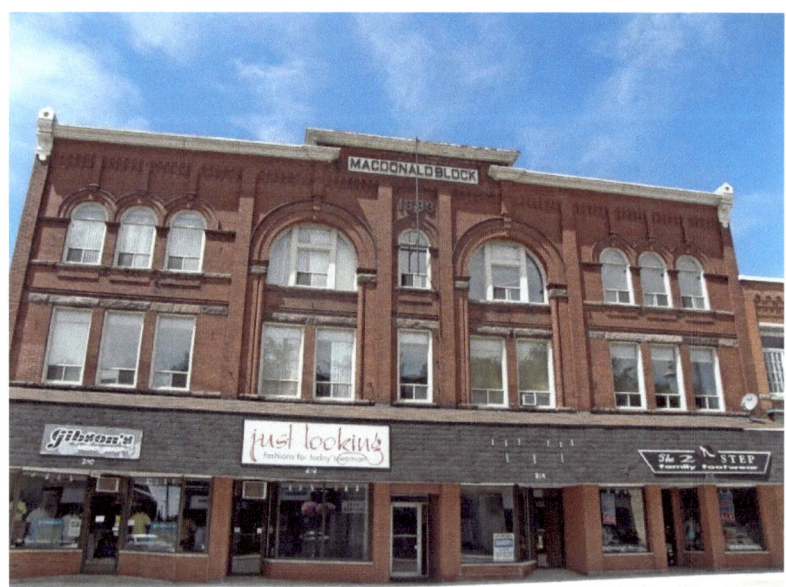

Romanesque style window arches, pilasters

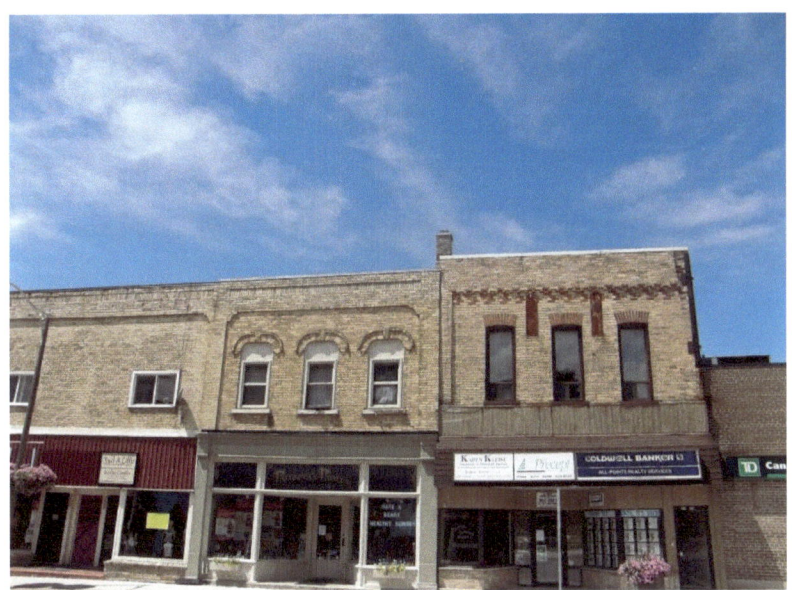

Window hoods, dichromatic brickwork

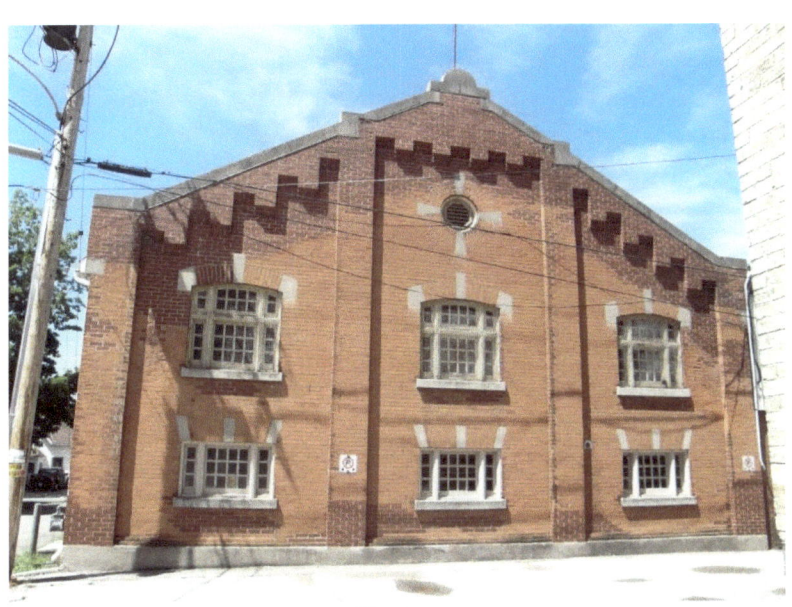

pilasters

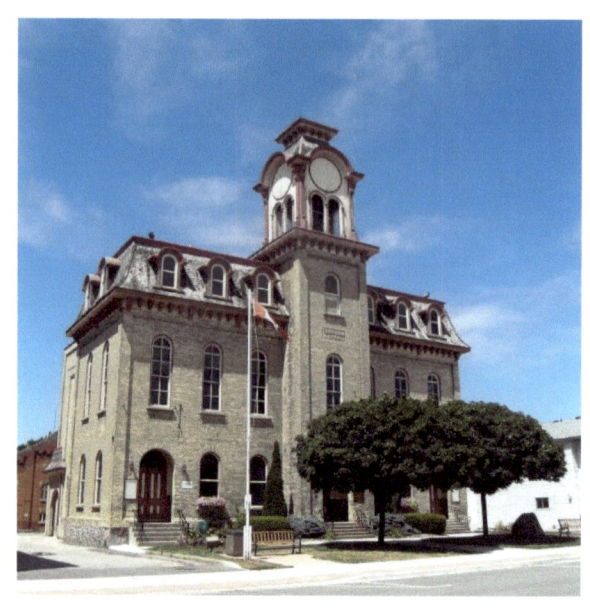

Town Hall A.D. 1890
Mansard roof, dormers, cornice brackets

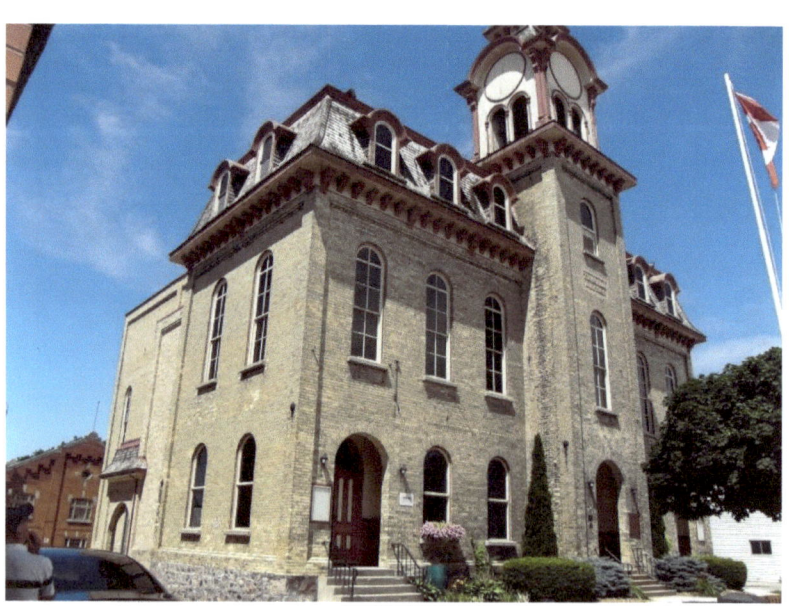

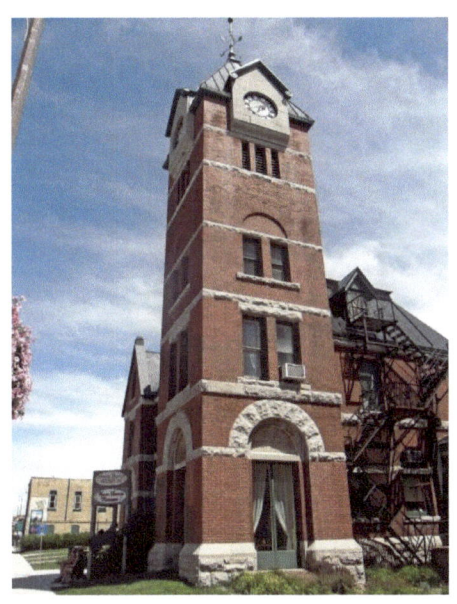

E.R. Post Office – Romanesque style

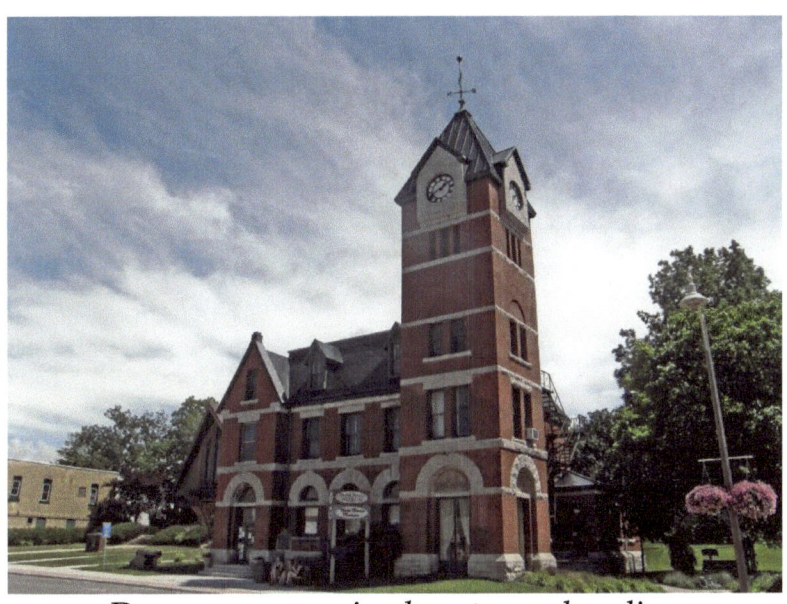

Dormers, voussoirs, keystones, banding

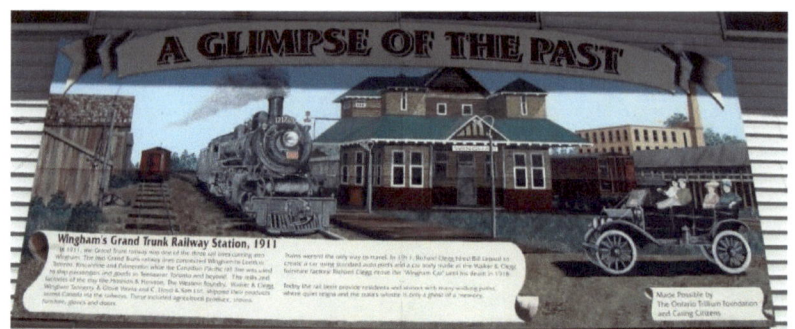

Wingham's Grand Trunk Railway Station

        In 1911, the Grand Trunk Railway was one of three
lines coming into Wingham. The two Grand Trunk railway
lines connected the town to London, Toronto, Kincardine, and
Palmerston. The Canadian Pacific rail line was used to ship
passengers and goods to Teeswater, Toronto and beyond. The
mills and factories of the day, like Howson & Howson, The
Western Founder, Walter Clegg, Wingham Tannery & Glove
Works, and C. Lloyd & Son Ltd. shipped their products across
Canada via the railways. The goods included agricultural
produce, stoves, furniture, gloves and doors.
        Trains weren't the only way to travel. In 1911, Richard
Clegg hired Bill Lepard to create a car using standard auto
parts and a car body made at the Walter & Clegg furniture
factory. Richard Clegg drove the "Wingham car" until his
death in 1918.
        Today the rail beds provide residents and visitors with
many walking paths where quiet reigns and the train's whistle
is only a ghost of a memory.

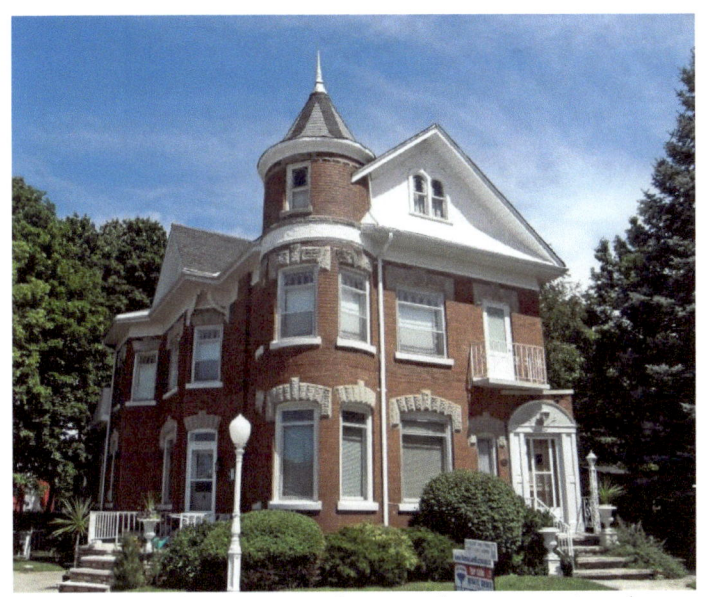

Queen Anne style – turret, fretwork, voussoirs, keystones

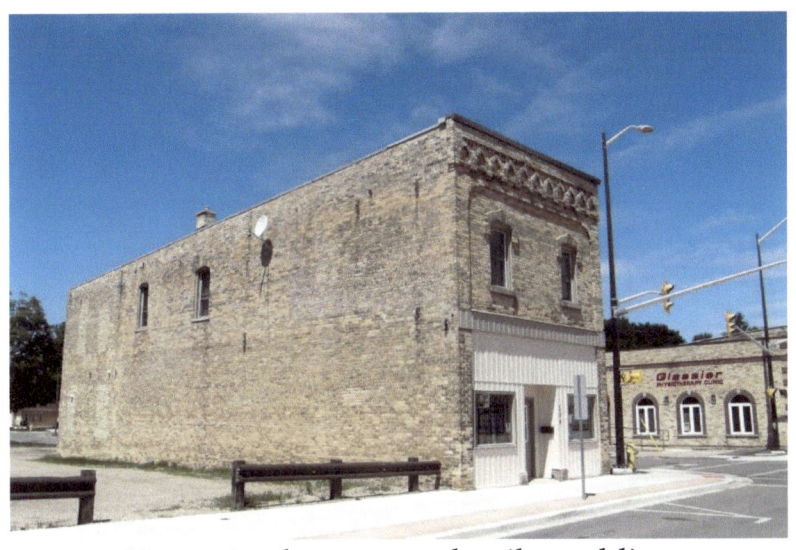

Voussoirs, keystones, dentil moulding

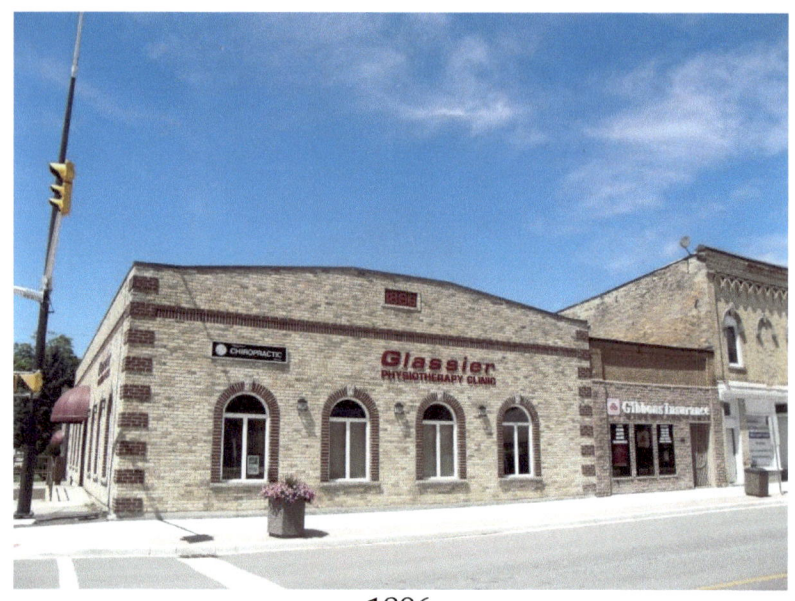

1896

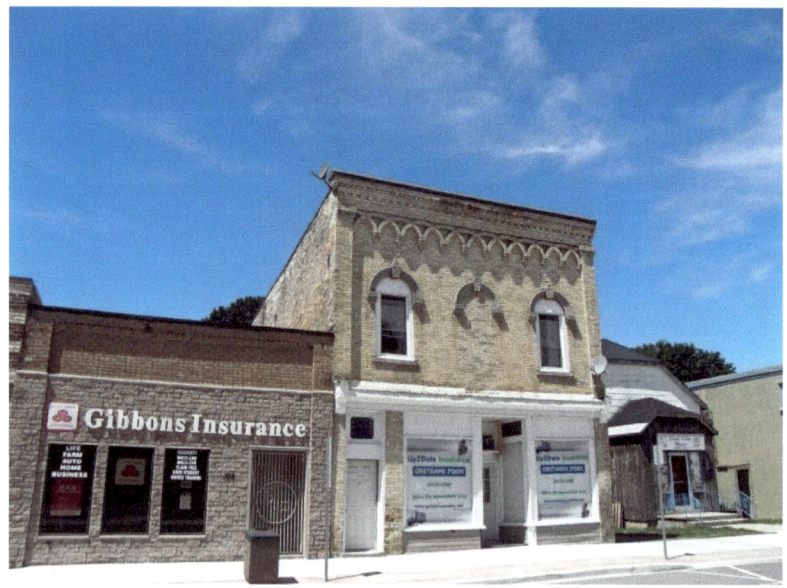

Dentil moulding, window hoods with keystones

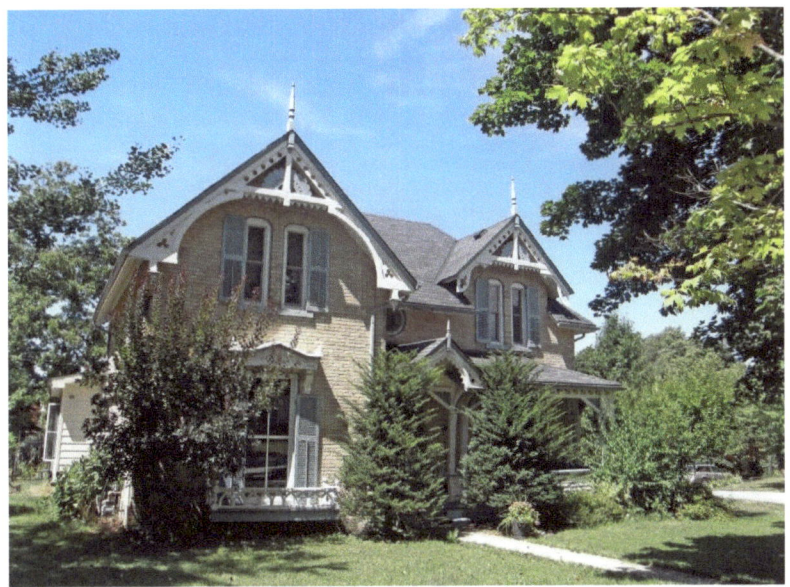

Gothic Revival – verge board trim and finial on gables

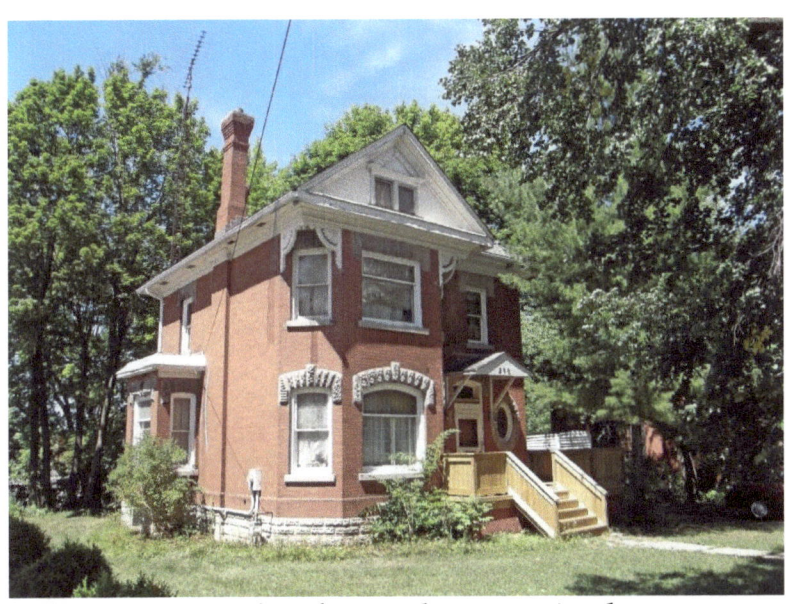

Edwardian style – fretwork, voussoirs, keystones

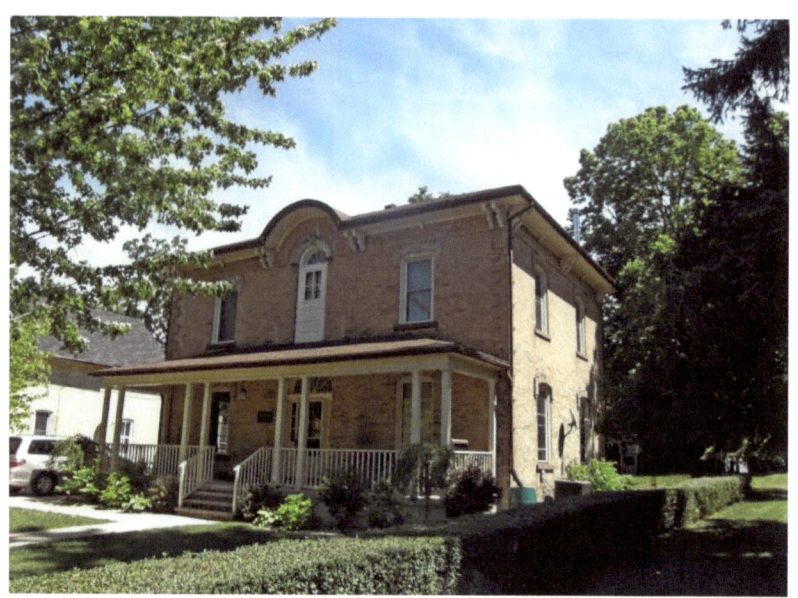

Italianate, cornice brackets

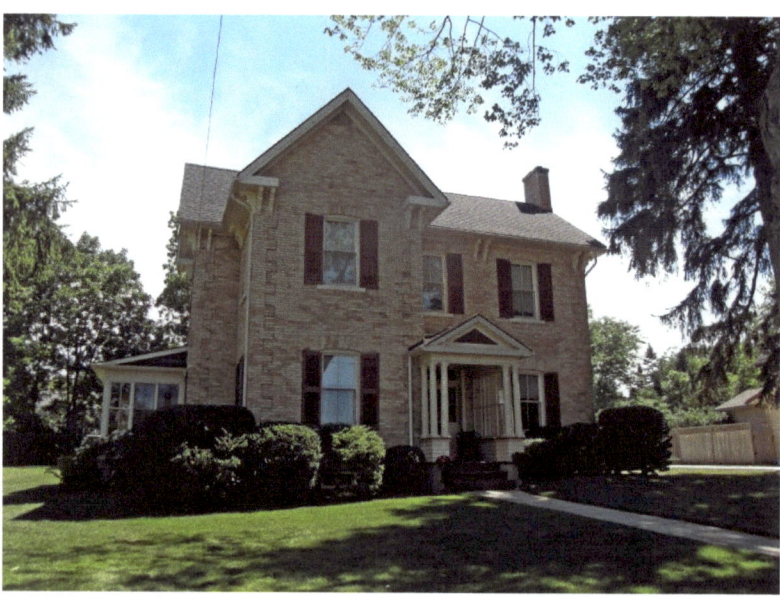

277 - Gothic Revival, cornice return on gable, cornice brackets, pediment above entranceway

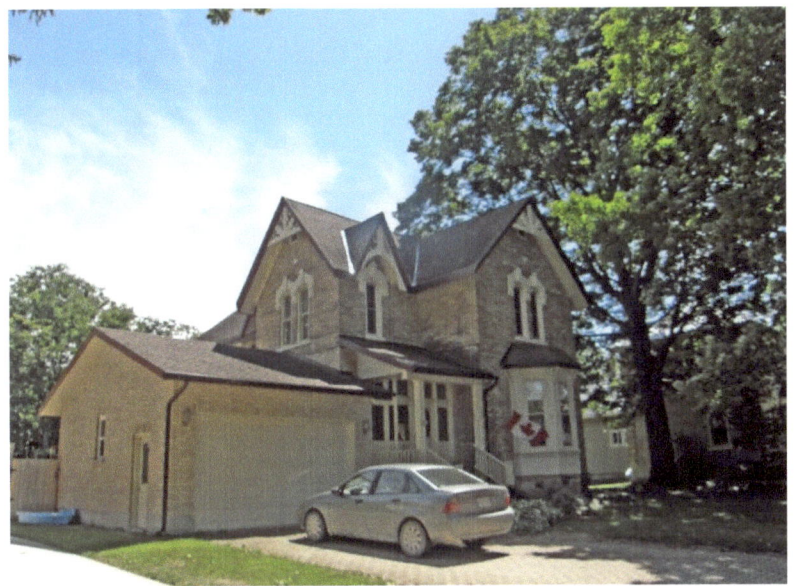

Gothic Revival, verge board trim

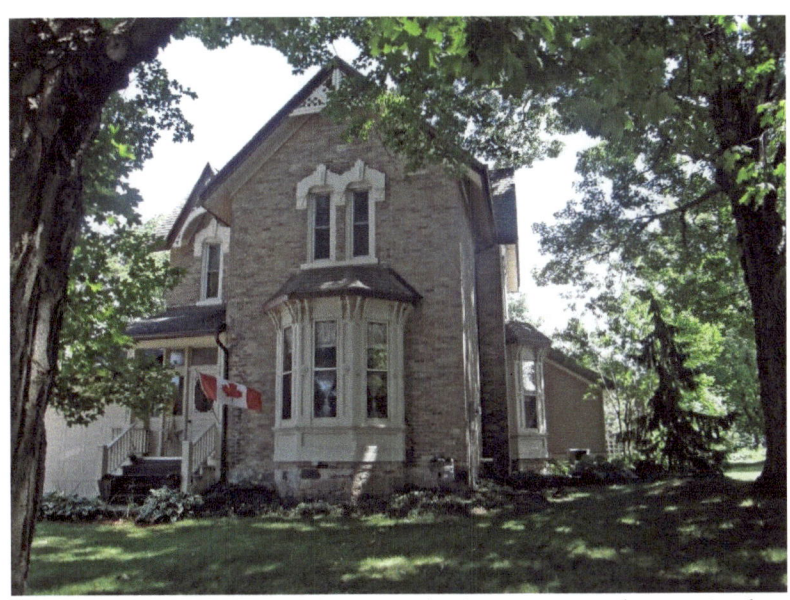

Gothic Revival - window hoods, keystones, bay window,
verge board trim on gable

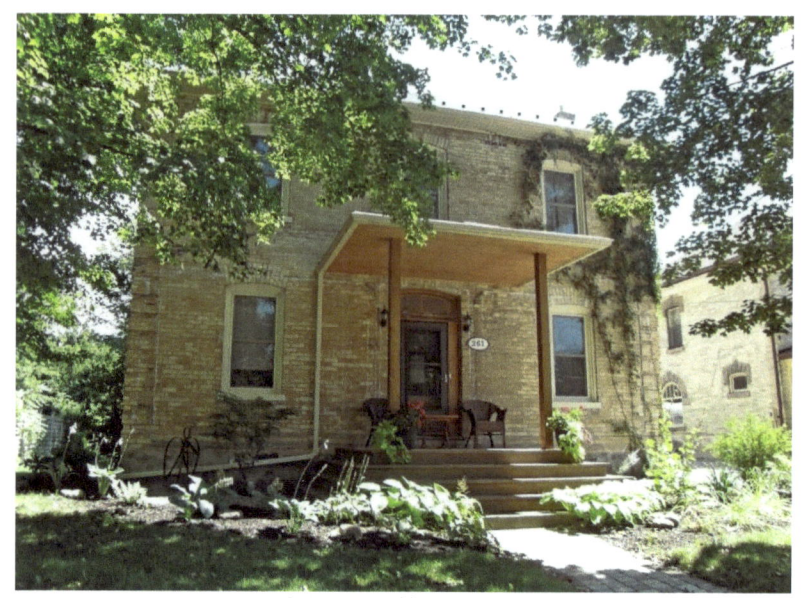

#261 - Yellow brick

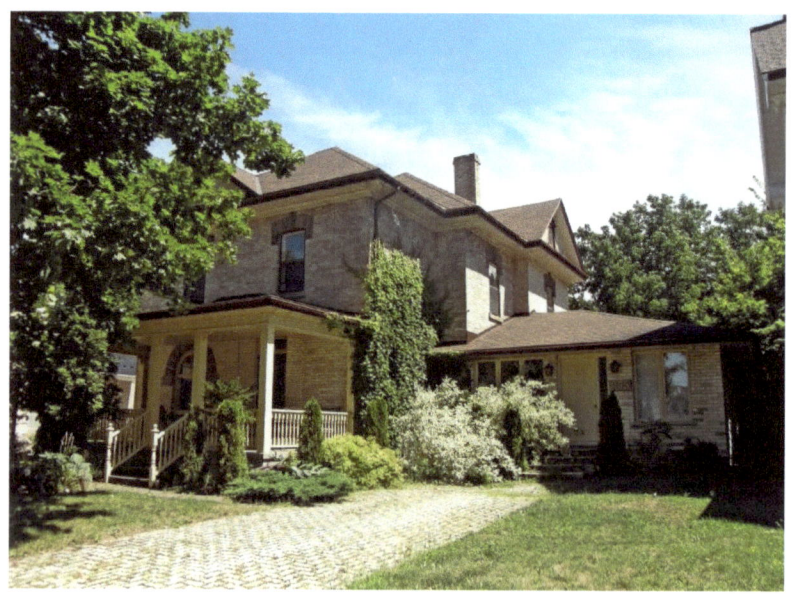

#255

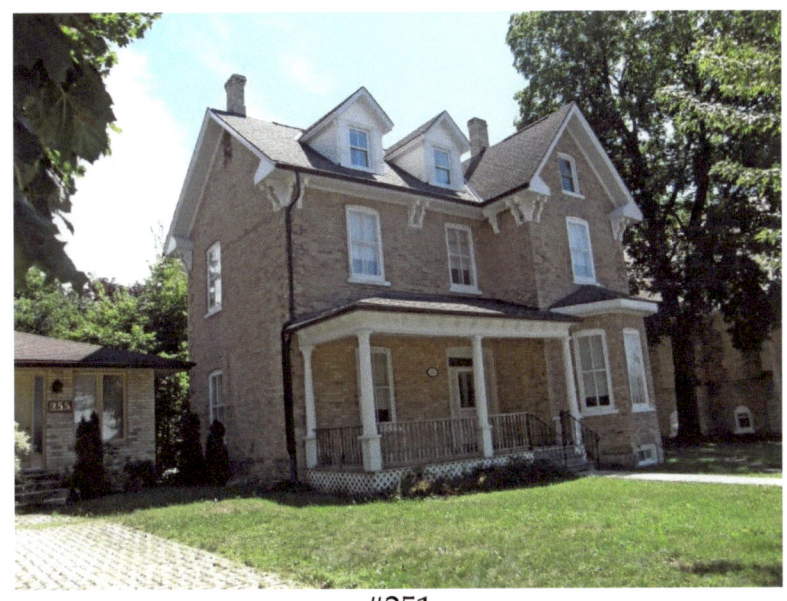

#251

Gothic Revival, dormers, cornice return, cornice brackets

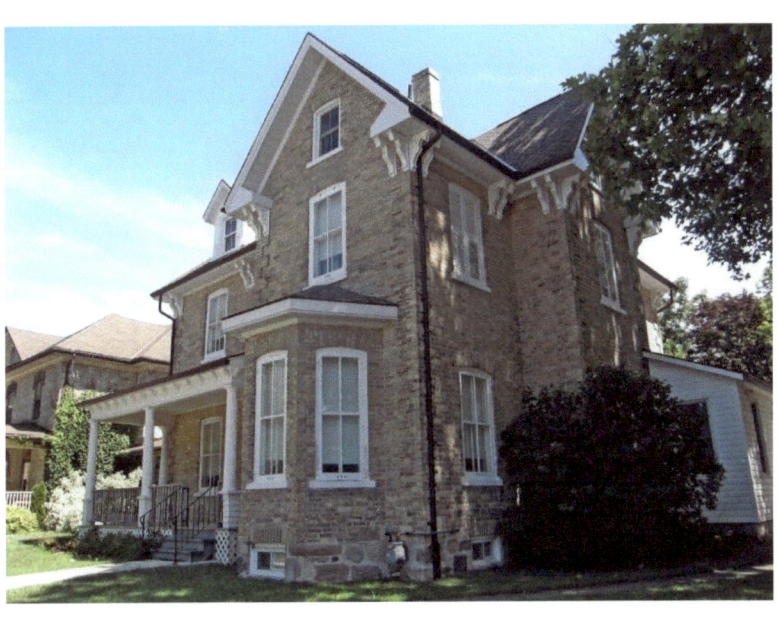

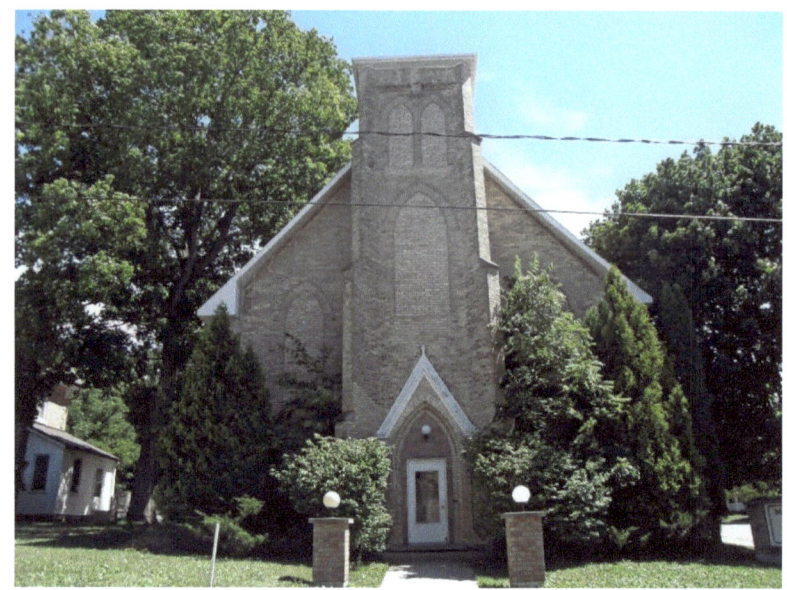

Masonic Lodge

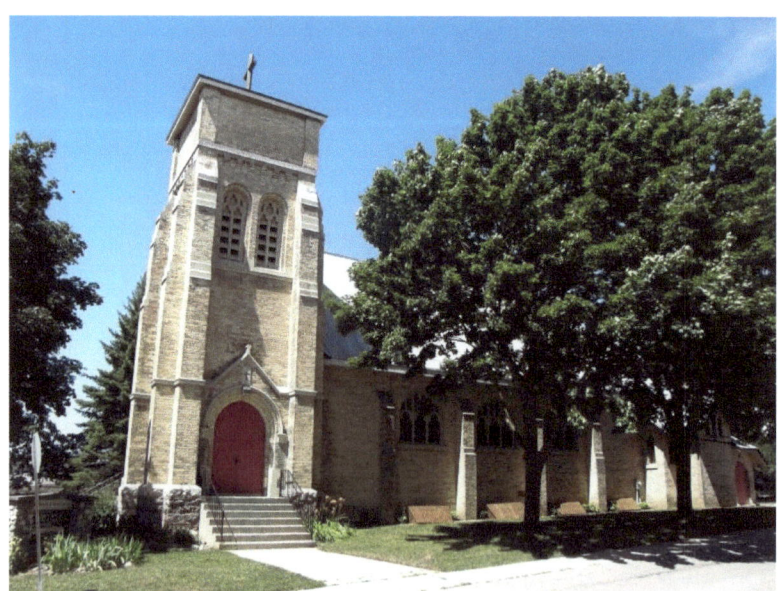

19 John Street East – St. Paul's Trinity Church, buttresses

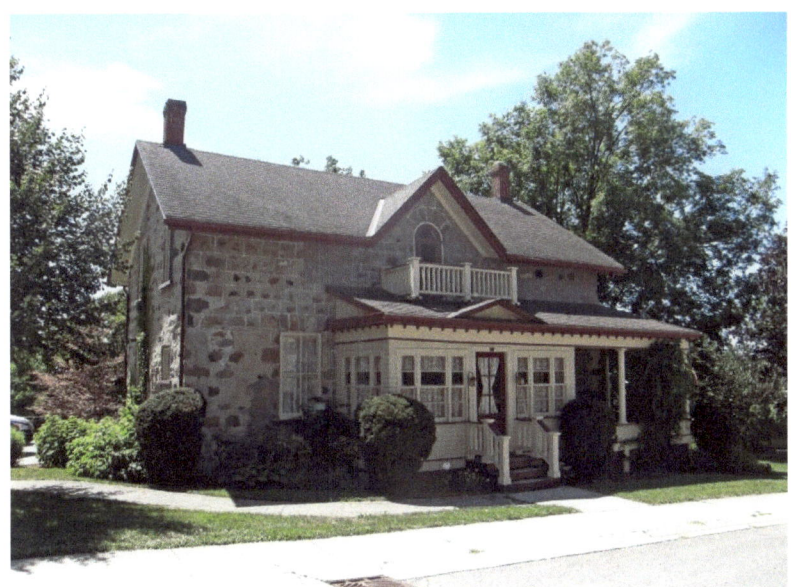

26 John Street East – cobblestone architecture, balcony on second floor

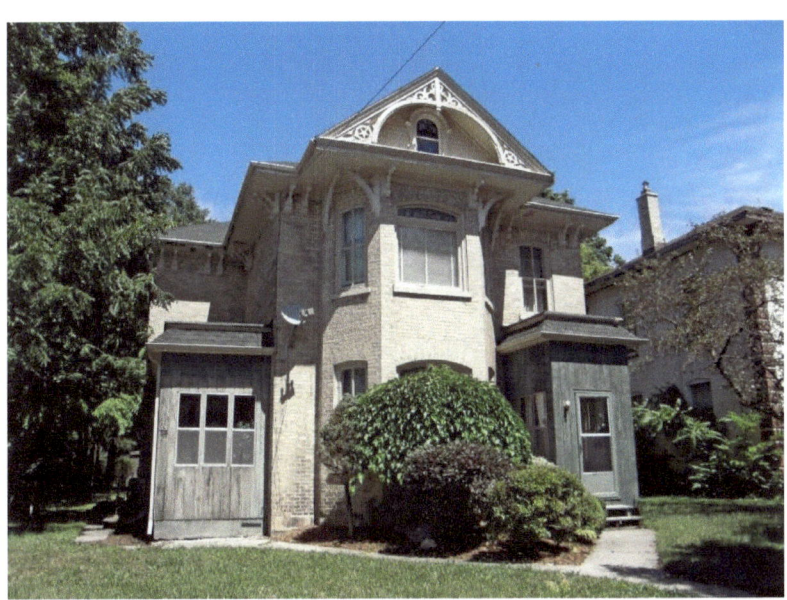

Verge board trim on gable, cornice brackets under eaves

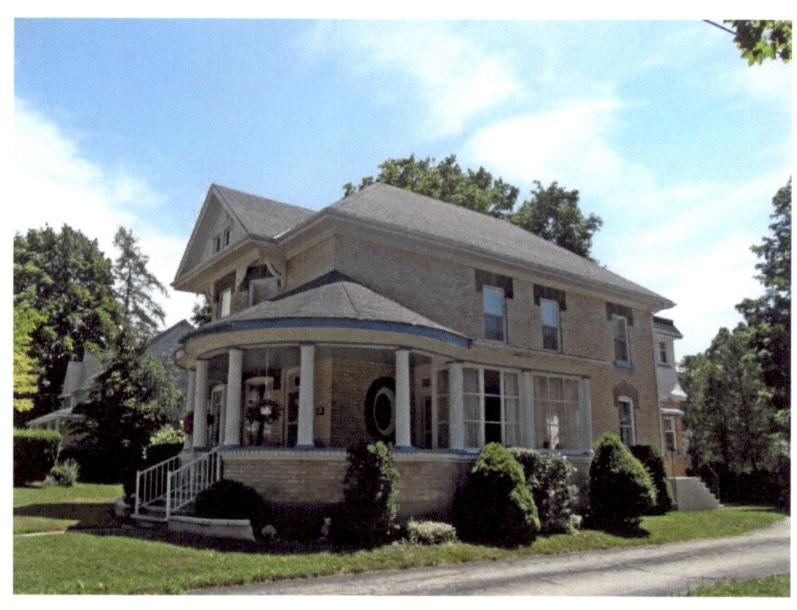

48 John Street East – Edwardian, fretwork, wraparound verandah

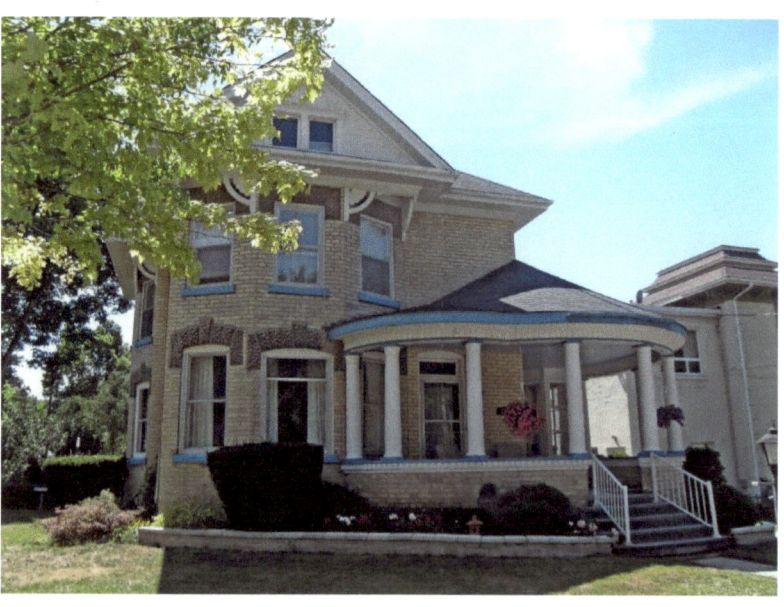

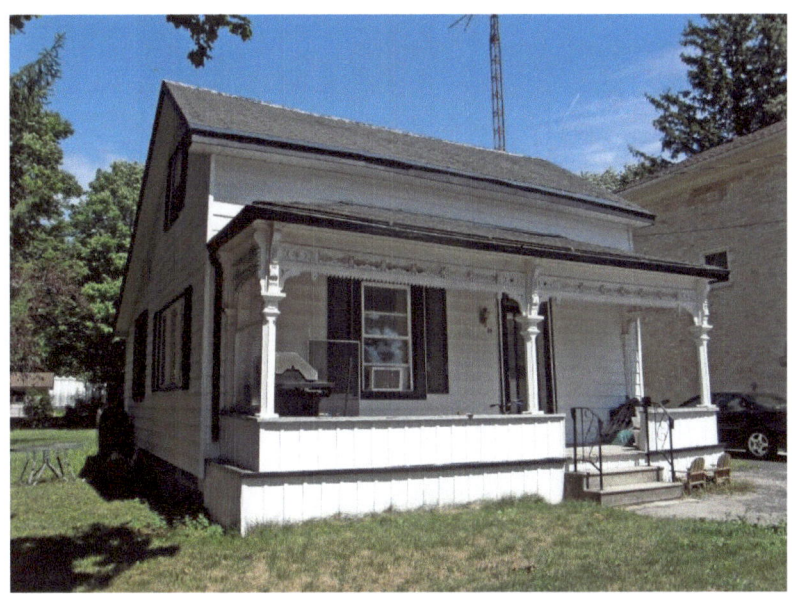

89 John Street East - saltbox

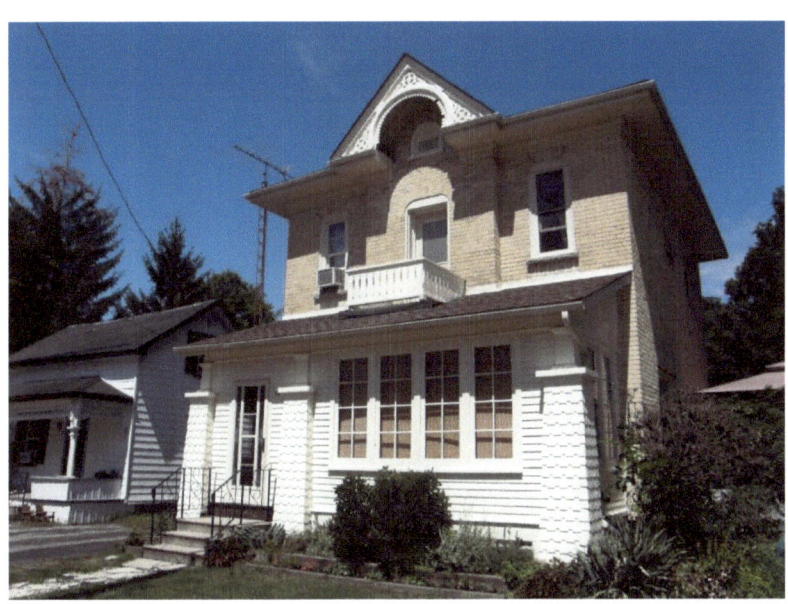

93 John Street East – verge board trim on gable, second floor balcony

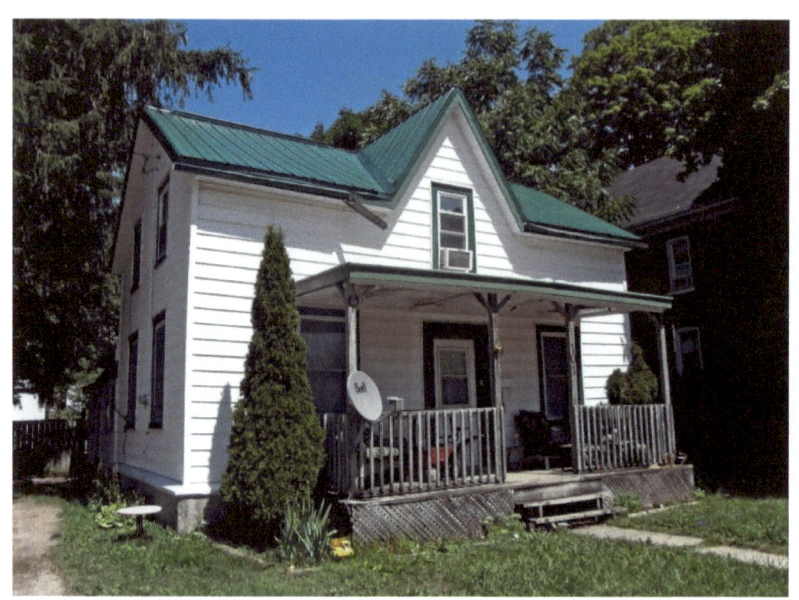

101 John Street East – Gothic Revival

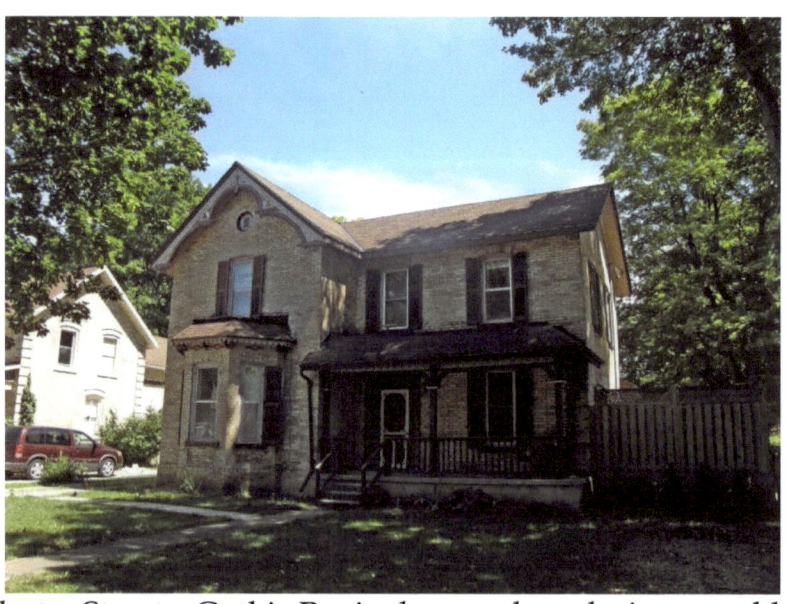

Shuter Street – Gothic Revival, verge board trim on gable,
bay window, yellow brick

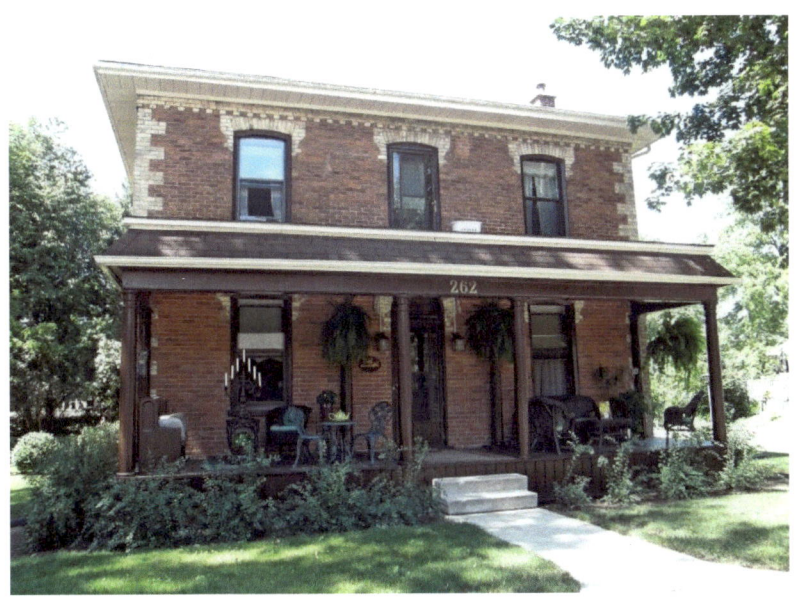

262 Shuter Street – Italianate, dichromatic brickwork

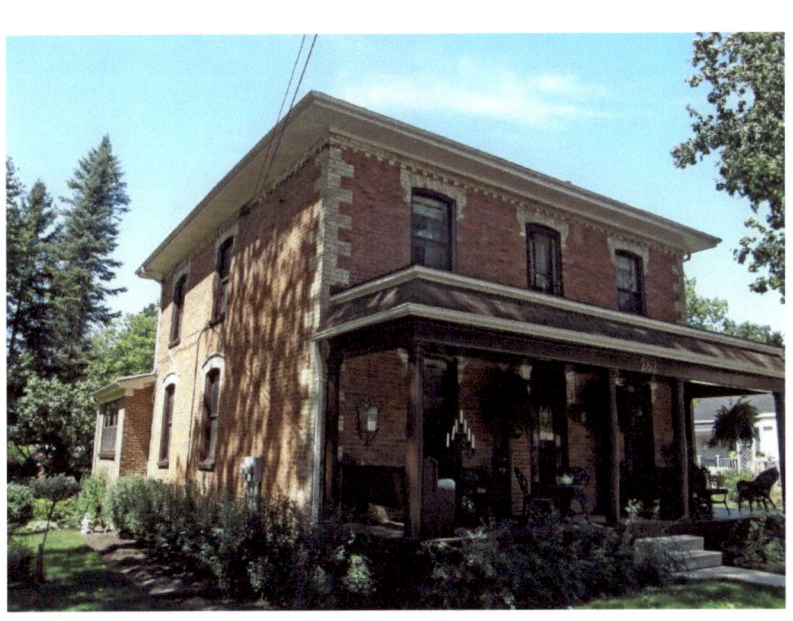

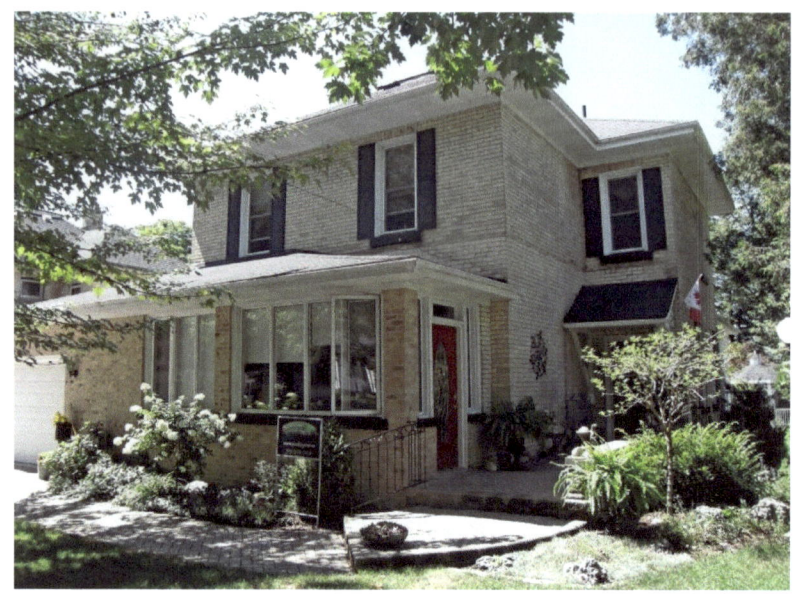

210 Shuter Street

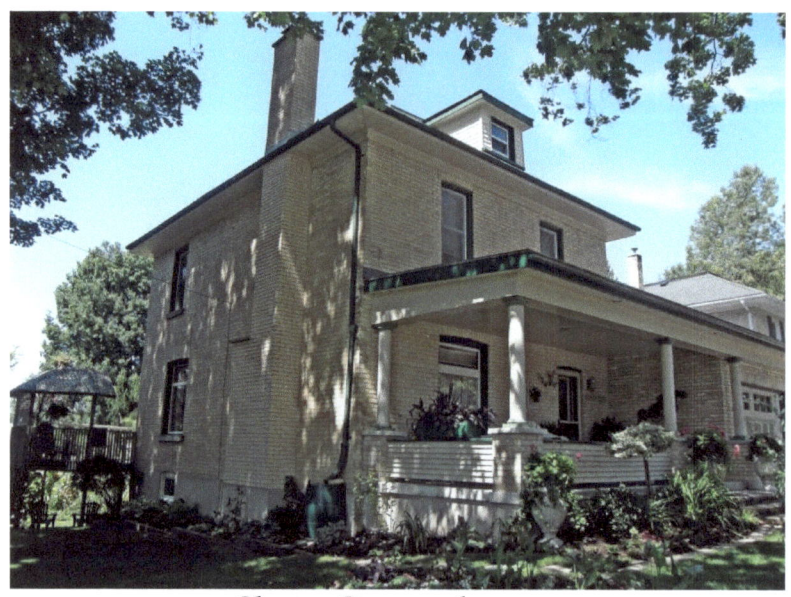

Shuter Street - dormer

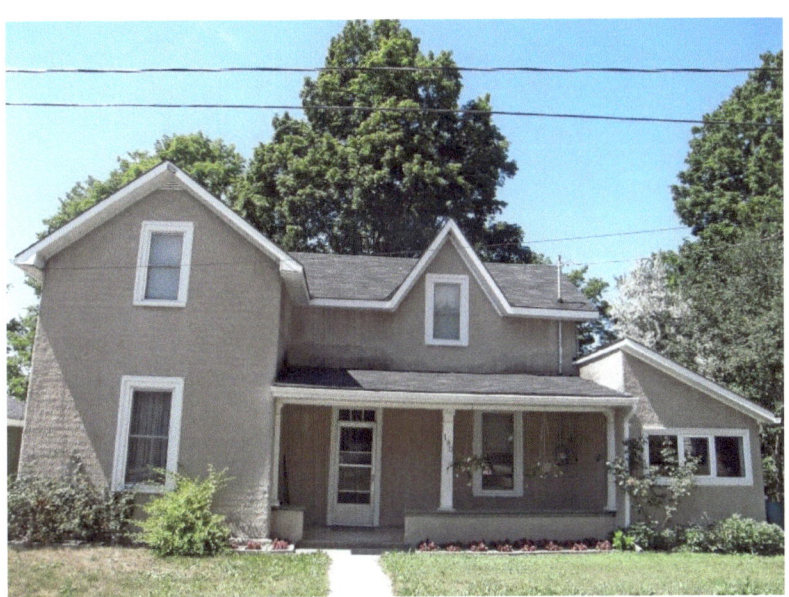

190 Shuter Street – Gothic Revival

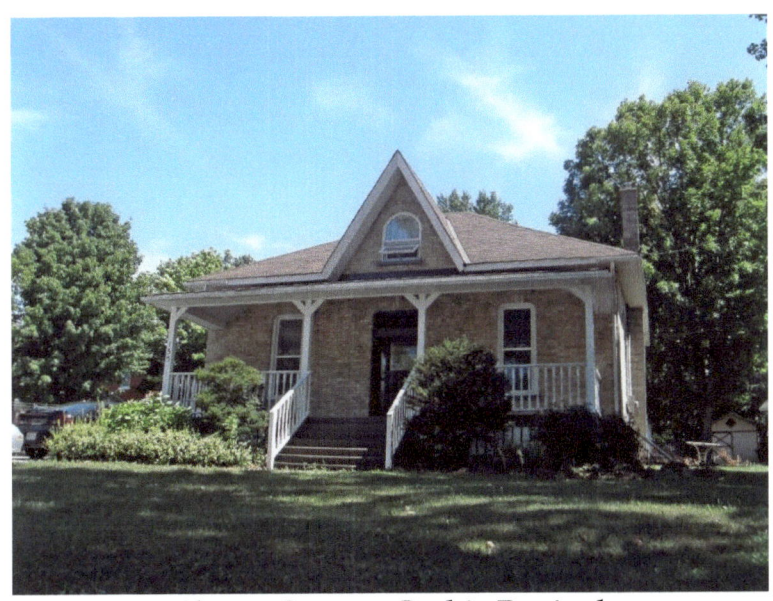

Shuter Street – Gothic Revival

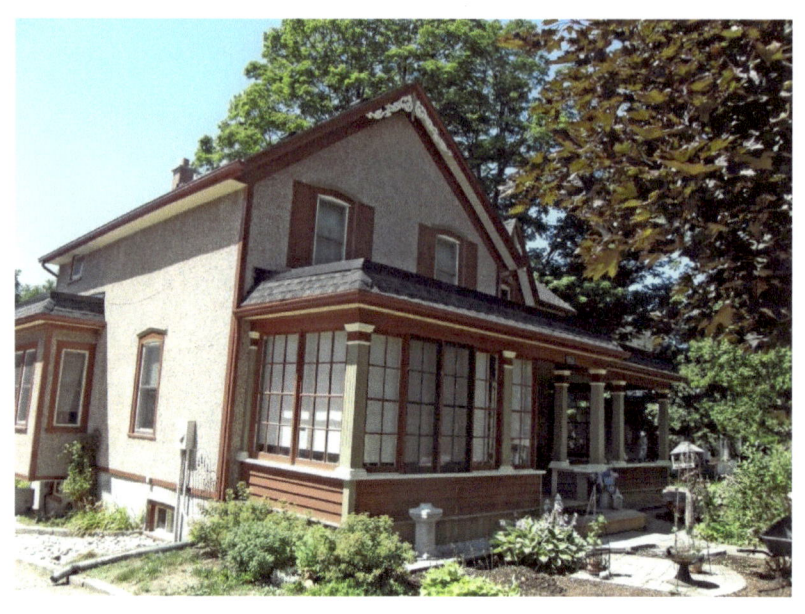

120 Shuter Street

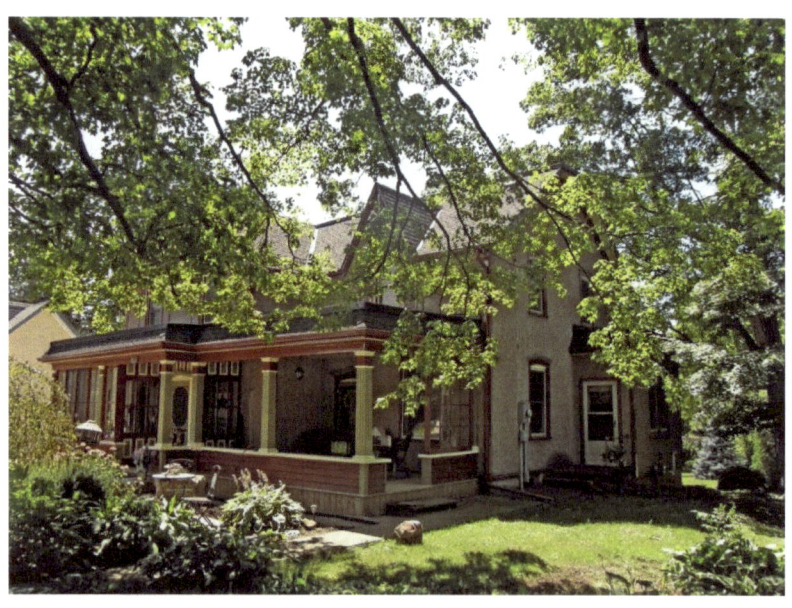

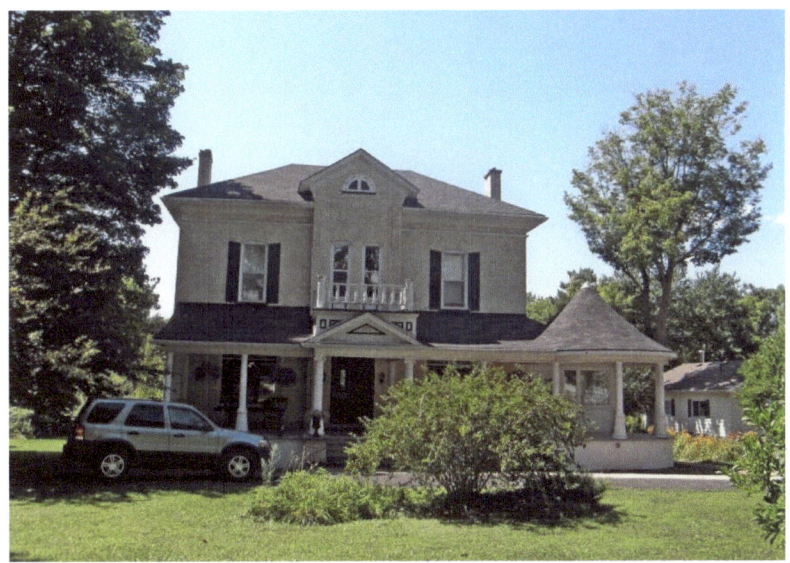

112 Shuter Street – Italianate, ionic capitals, two-and-a-half storey tower-like bay, second floor balcony

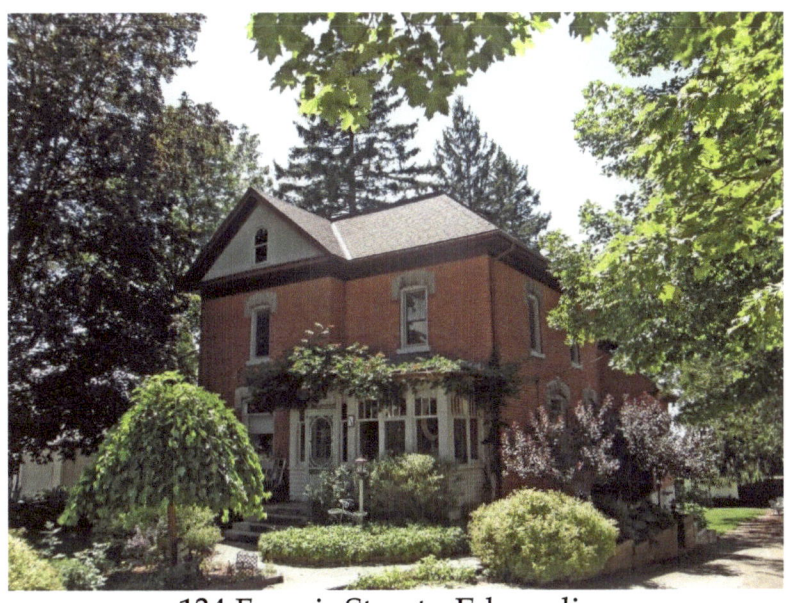

134 Francis Street - Edwardian

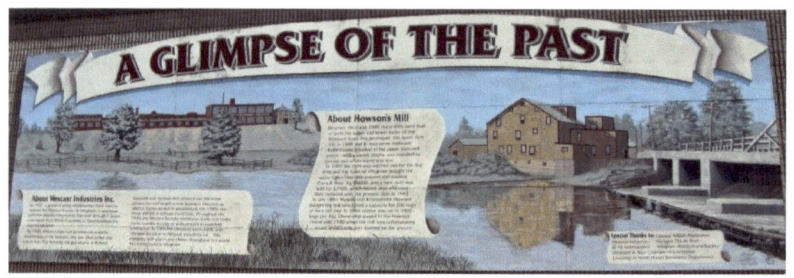

Howson's Mill

Between 1862 and 1888 many mills were built at both the upper and lower dams of the Maitland River. Fire destroyed the lower dam mill in 1888 and it was never replaced. Rollers were installed in the upper dam mill and in 1895 a steam engine was installed to run the mill when the water was low. In 1899 the dam was washed out for the third time and the Town of Wingham bought the water rights from the present mill owners Carrs & Bros. for $4,000 and a new dam was built for $3,500 which lasted until 1921. The present dam was built in 1982.

In late 1899 Harvey and Brocklebank Howson bought the mill which had a capacity of 200 bags of flour per day. In 1944 output was up to 1,000 bags per day.

Ownership stayed in the Howson name until 1950 when the mill was struck by lightning and burned to the ground.

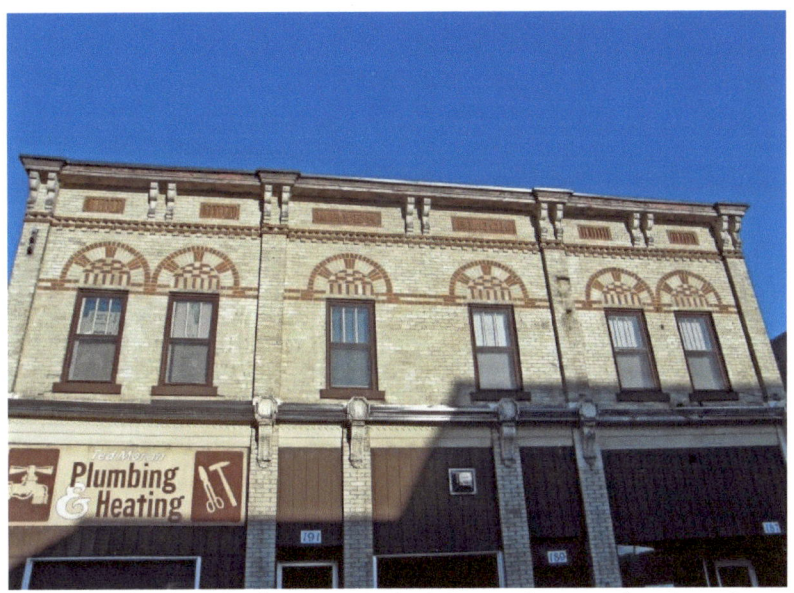

Meyer Block - dichromatic brickwork, cornice brackets

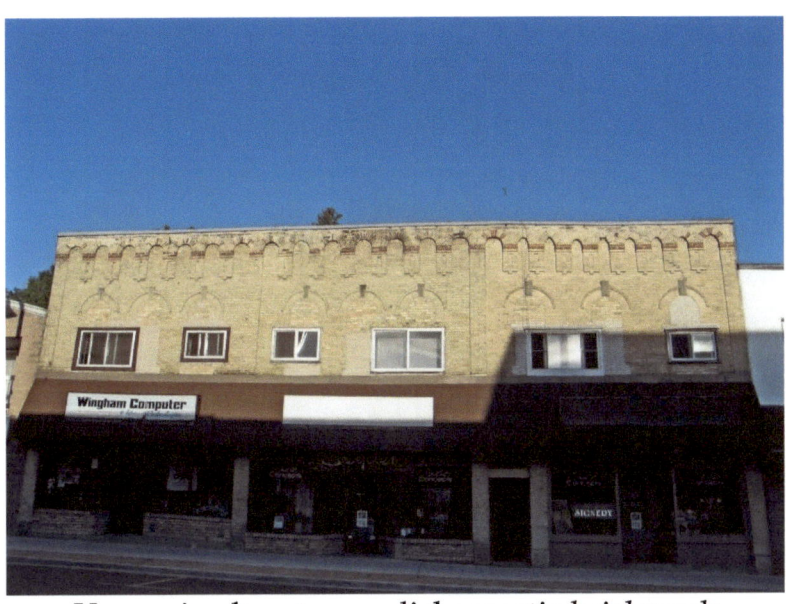

Voussoirs, keystones, dichromatic brickwork

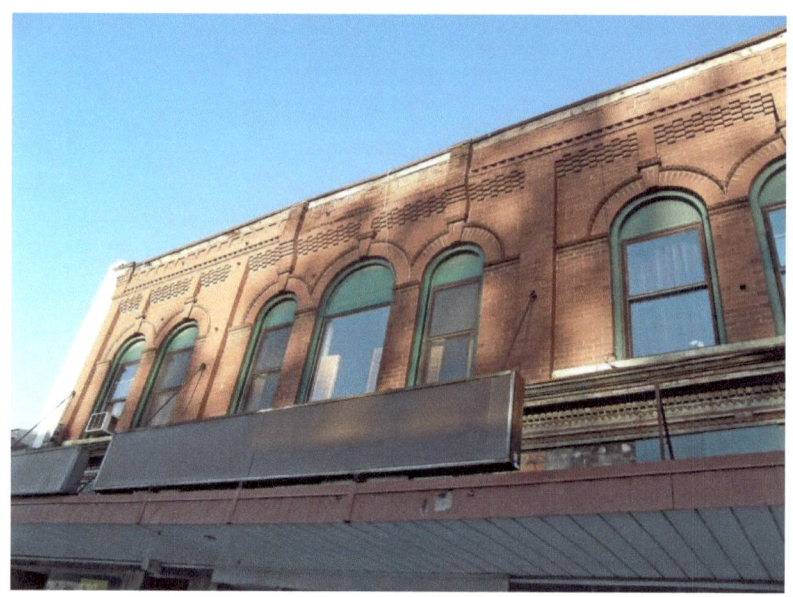

Bevelled dentil moulding

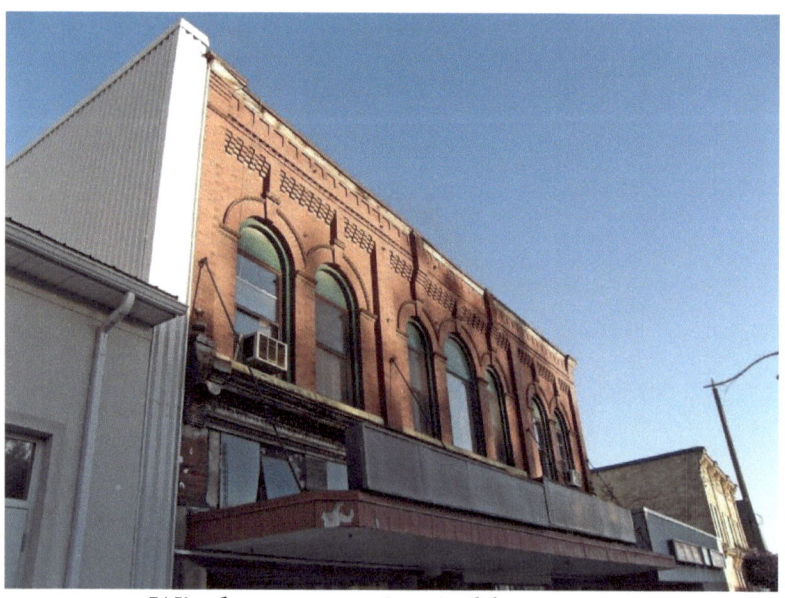

Window voussoirs and keystones

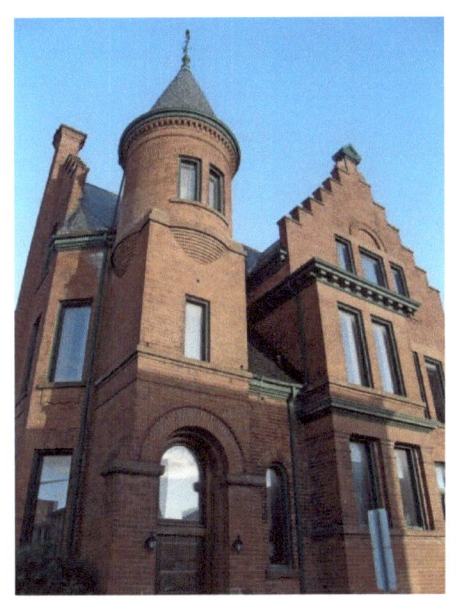

#221 – Queen Anne style, turret

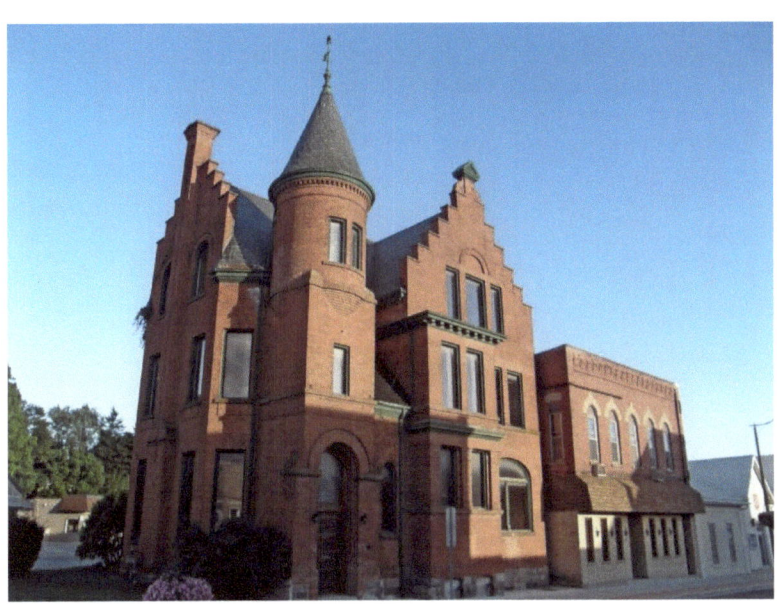

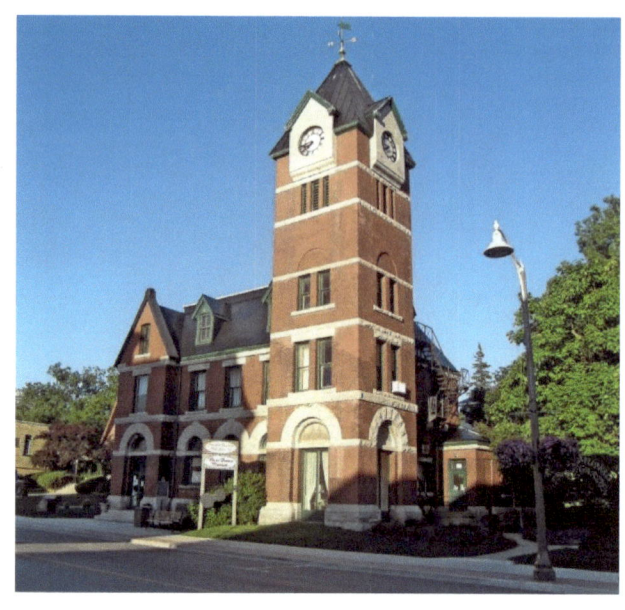

E. R. Post Office – Romanesque window arches

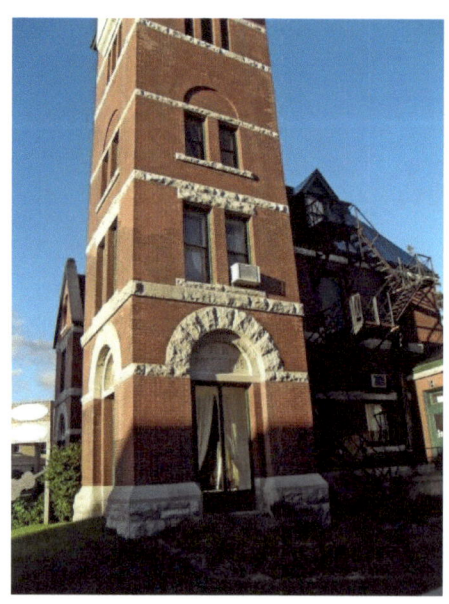

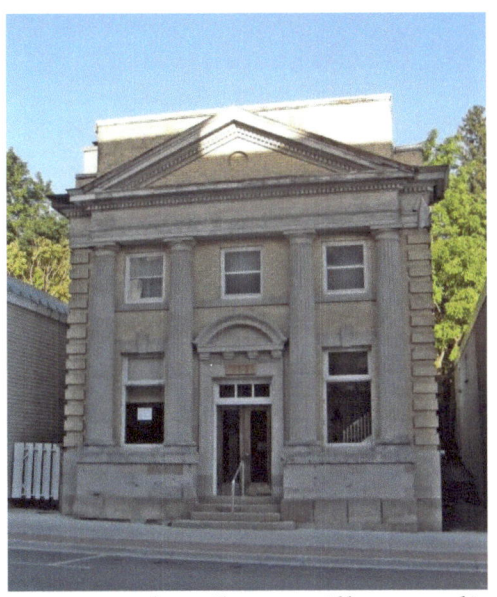

#253 - Beaux Arts style, pilaster pillars, pediment, dentil
moulding in tympanum, corner quoins

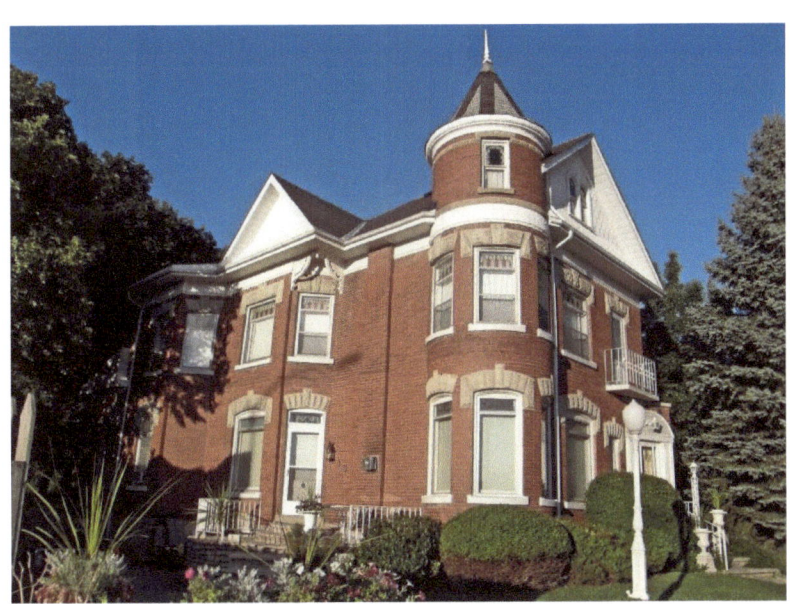

#13 - Queen Anne style, turret, voussoirs, keystones, fretwork

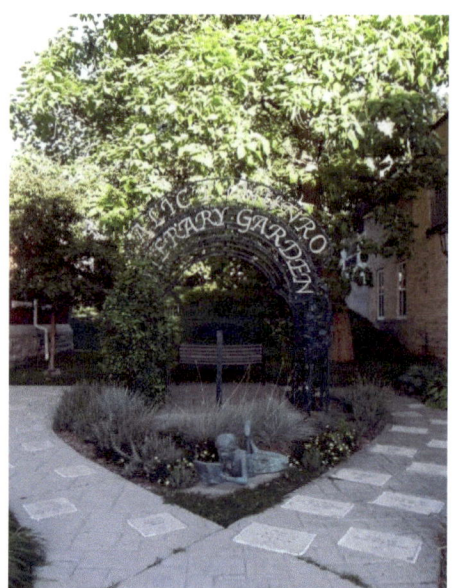

Alice Munro Literary Garden

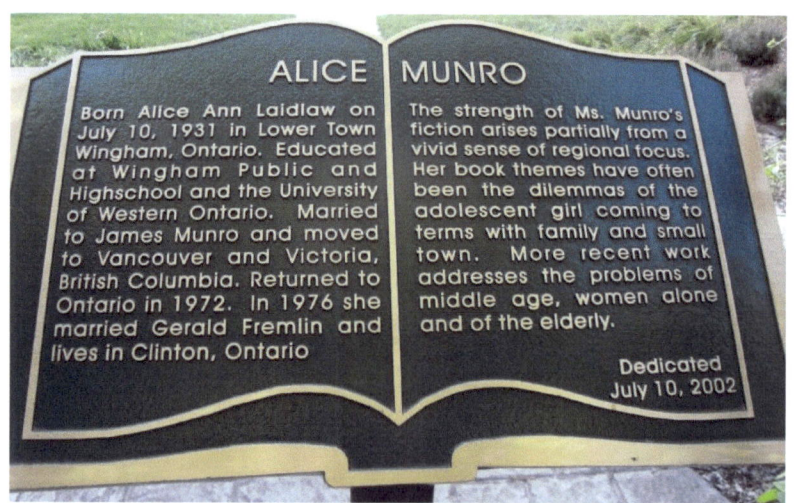

ALICE MUNRO

Born Alice Ann Laidlaw on July 10, 1931 in Lower Town Wingham, Ontario. Educated at Wingham Public and Highschool and the University of Western Ontario. Married to James Munro and moved to Vancouver and Victoria, British Columbia. Returned to Ontario in 1972. In 1976 she married Gerald Fremlin and lives in Clinton, Ontario

The strength of Ms. Munro's fiction arises partially from a vivid sense of regional focus. Her book themes have often been the dilemmas of the adolescent girl coming to terms with family and small town. More recent work addresses the problems of middle age, women alone and of the elderly.

Dedicated
July 10, 2002

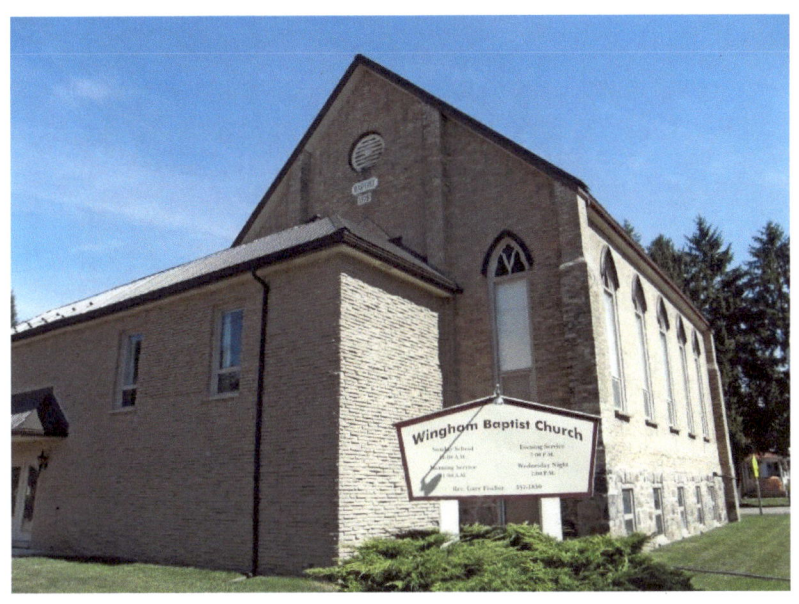

Wingham Baptist Church 1876 – Gothic Revival

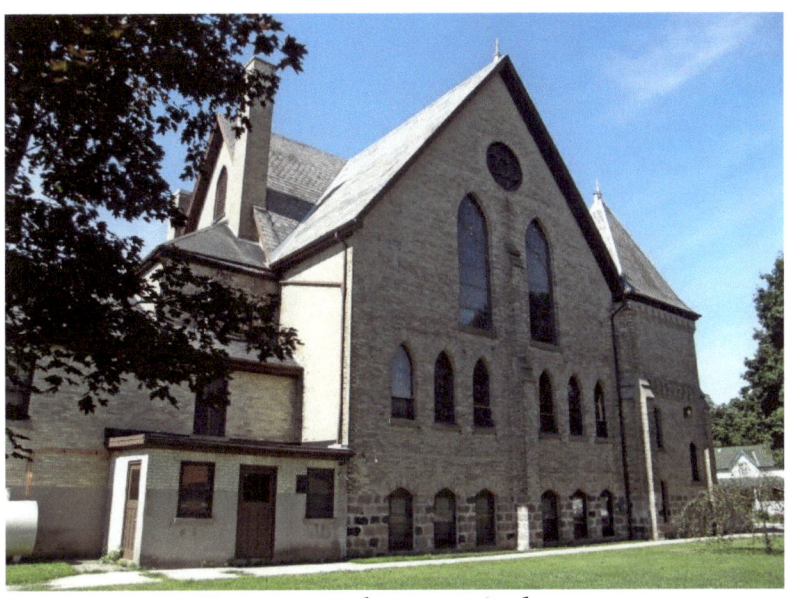

Buttresses, lancet windows

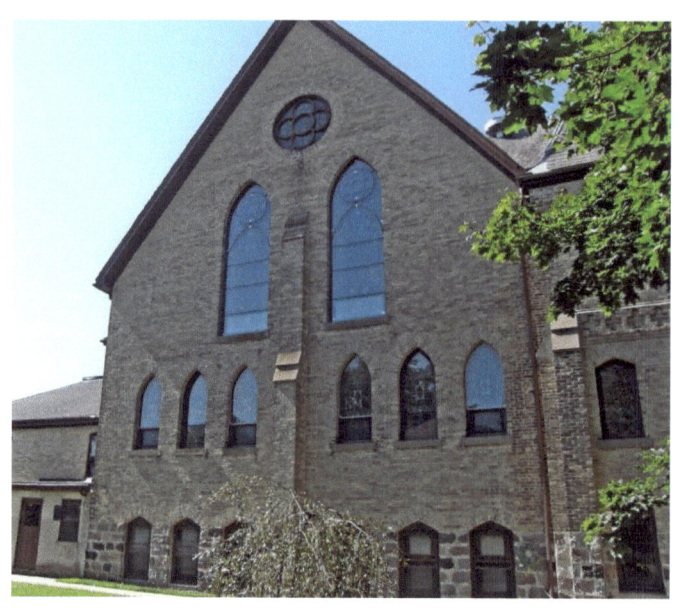

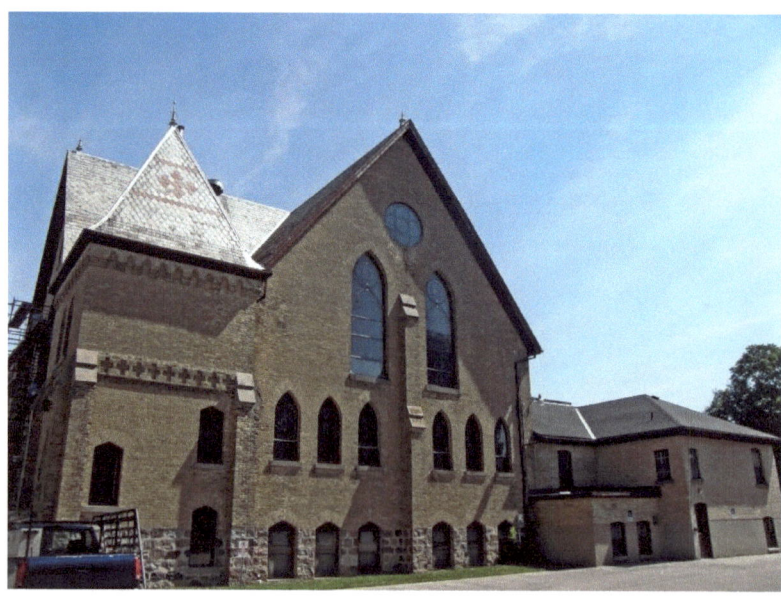

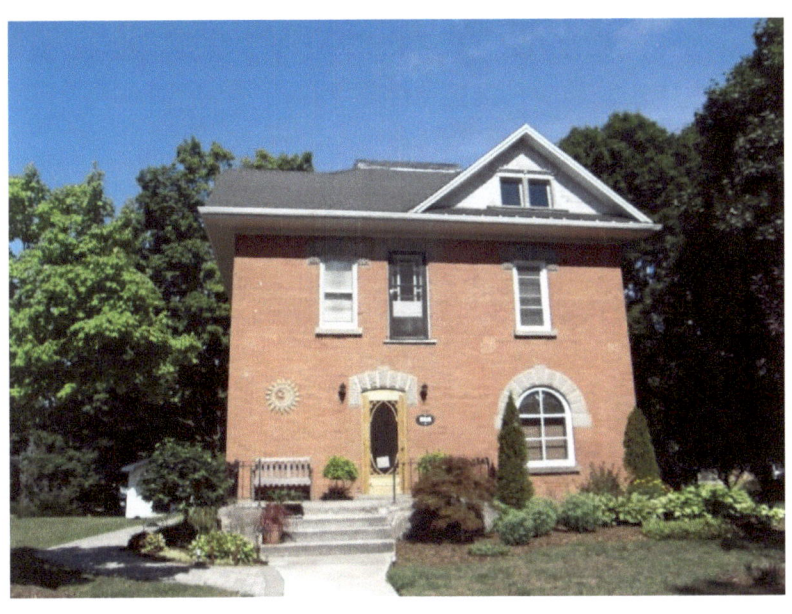

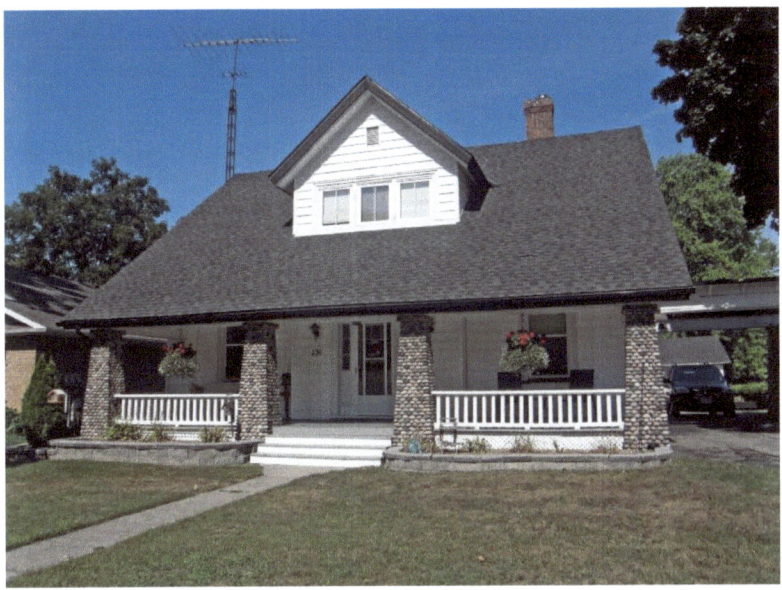

Dormer in attic

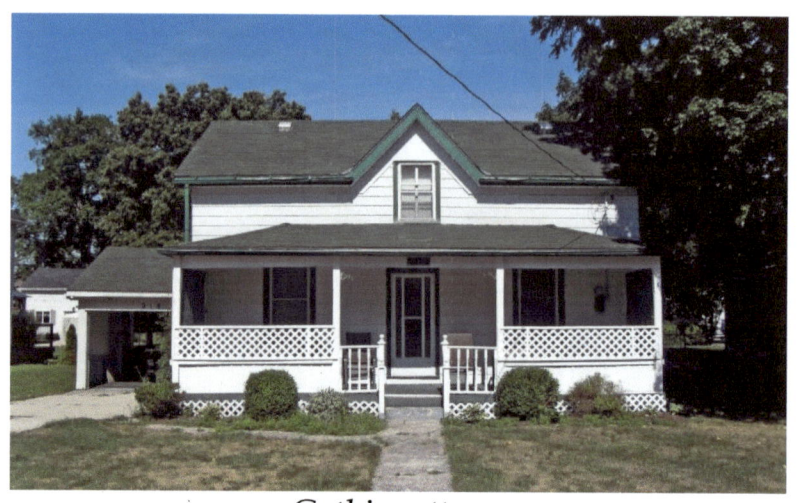

Gothic cottage

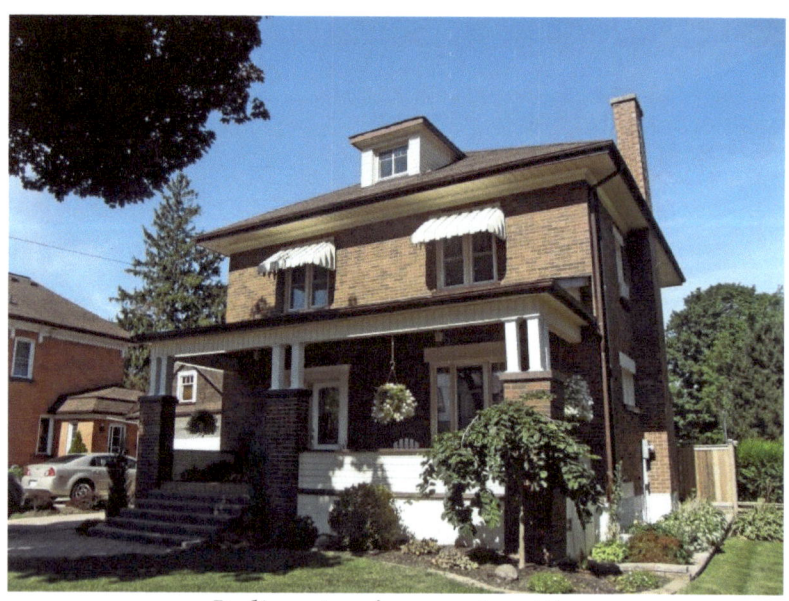

Italianate, dormer in attic

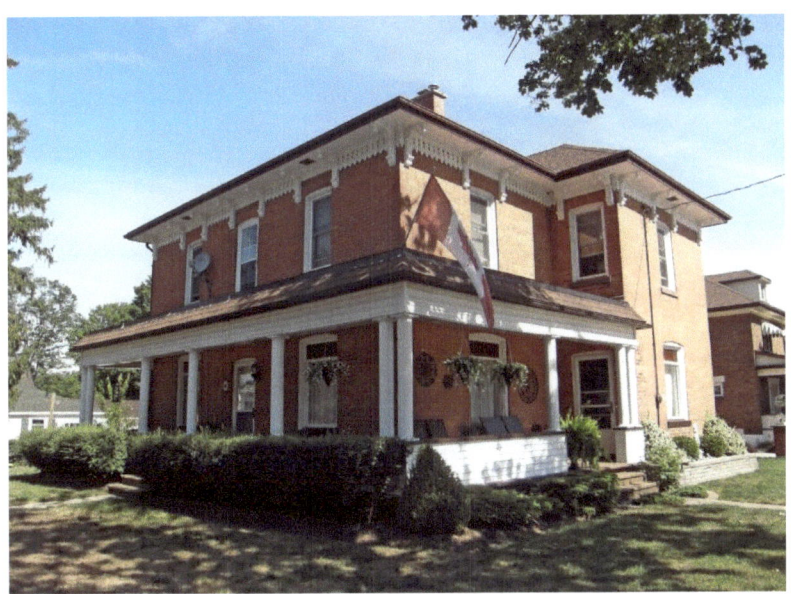

#69 - Italianate, cornice brackets, wraparound verandah, decorative cornice

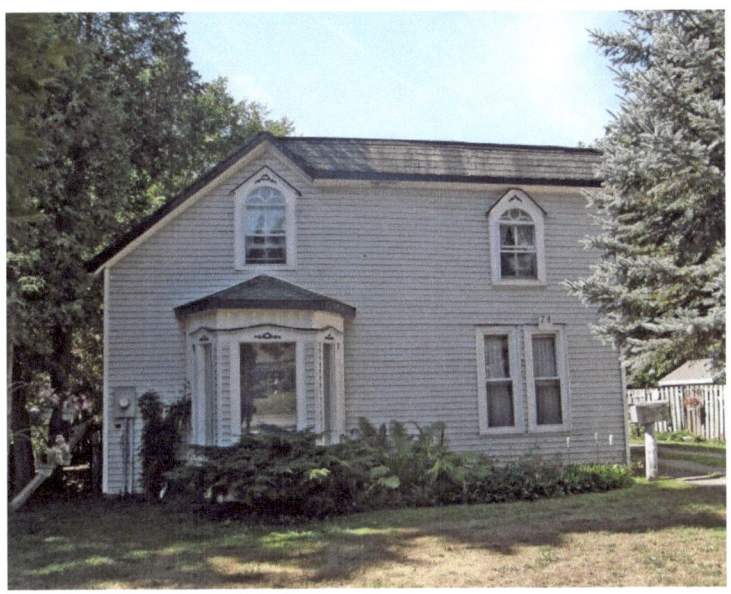

Bay window

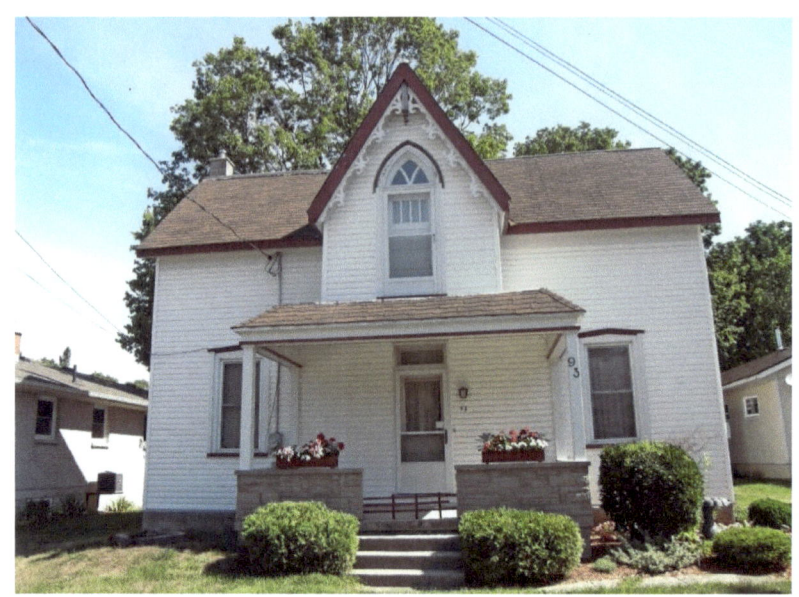

#93 - Gothic Revival, verge board trim on gable

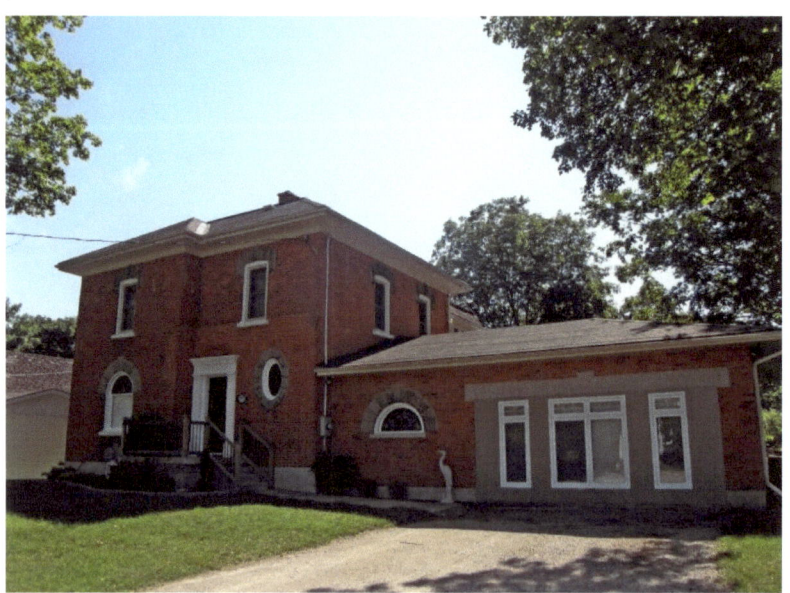

#199 - Italianate, hipped roof

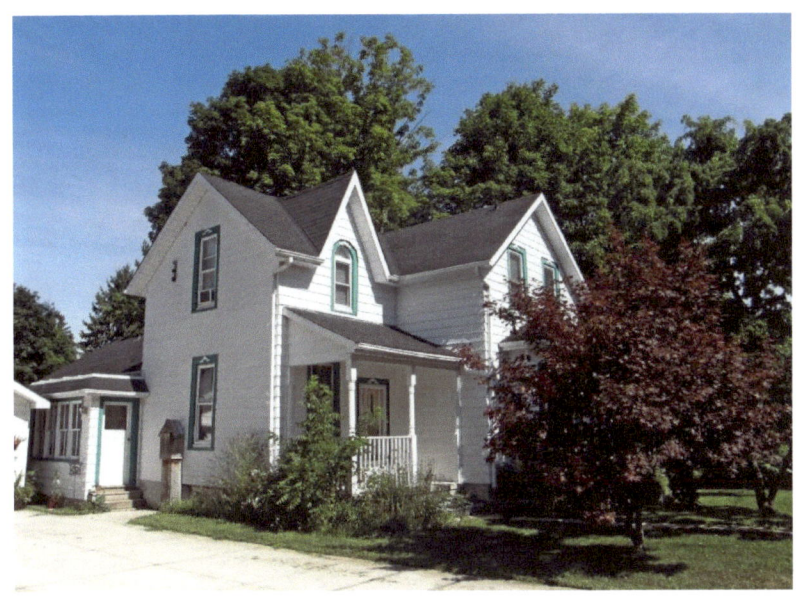

Gothic Revival, bay window

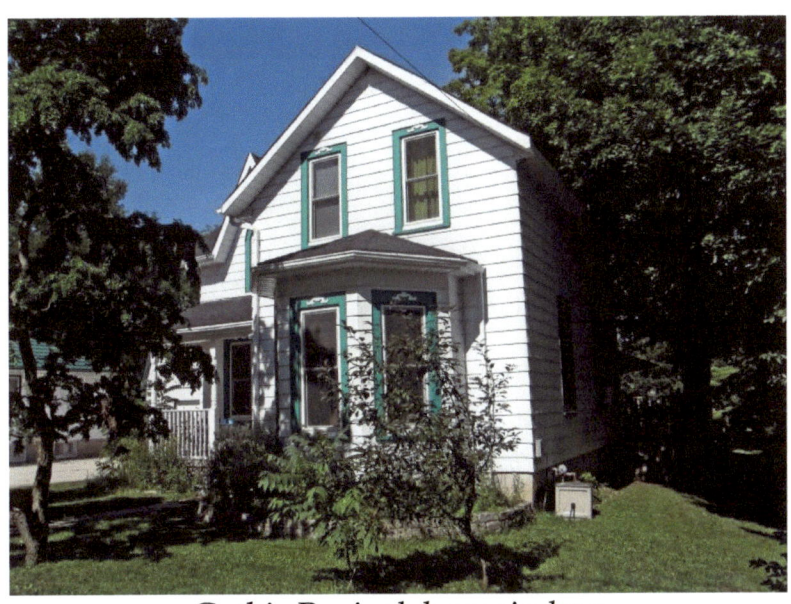

Gothic Revival, bay window

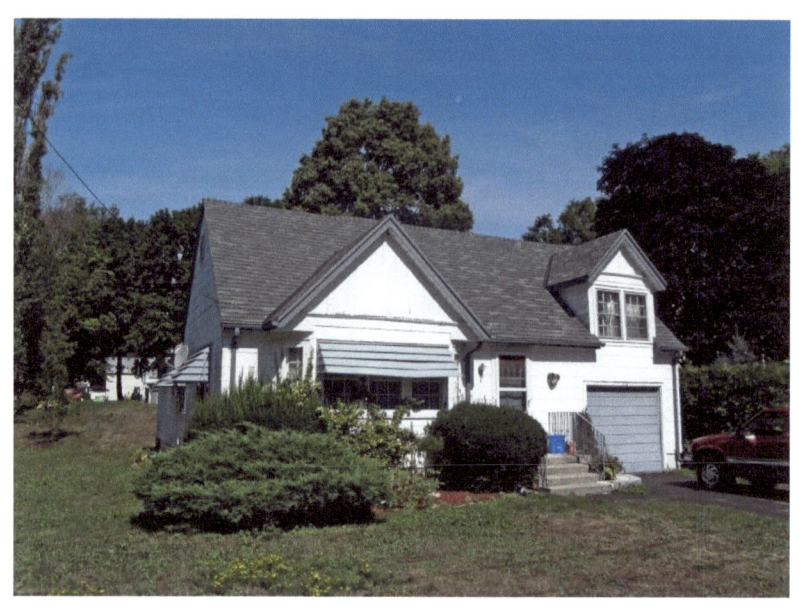

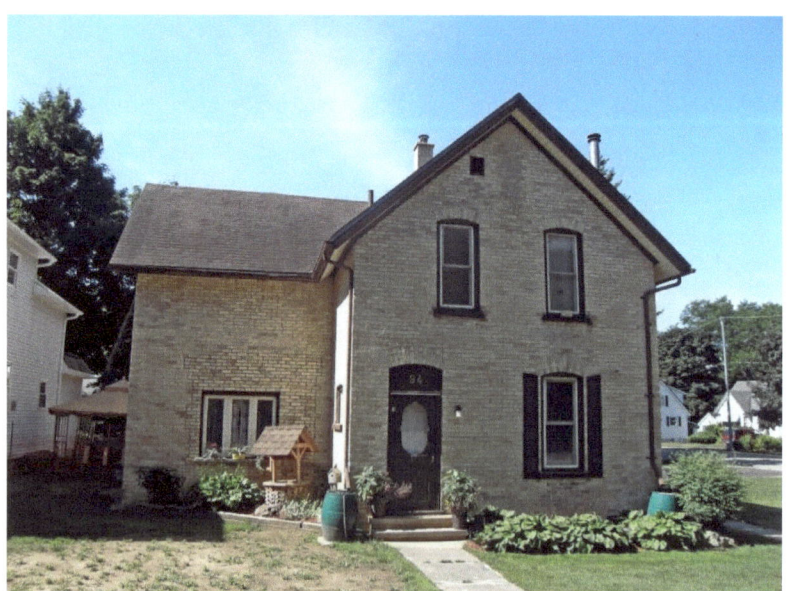

#94 - Gothic Revival

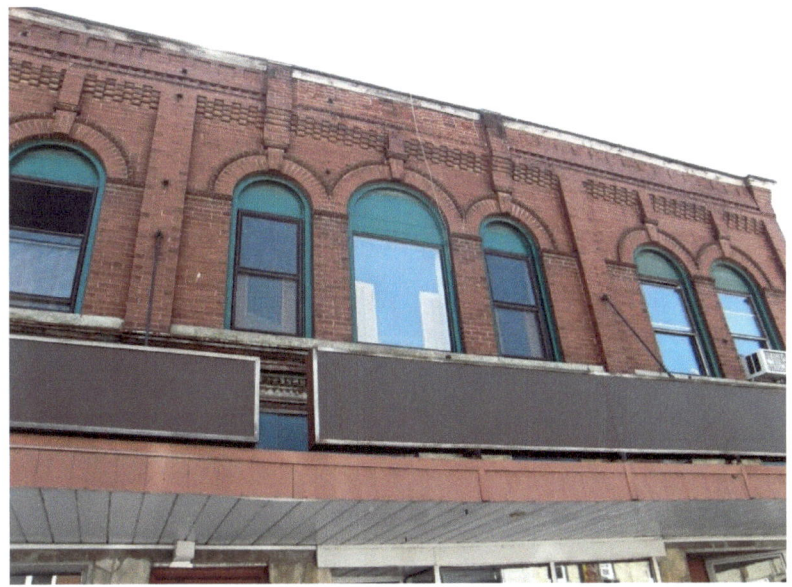

Bevelled dentil moulding, voussoirs and keystones

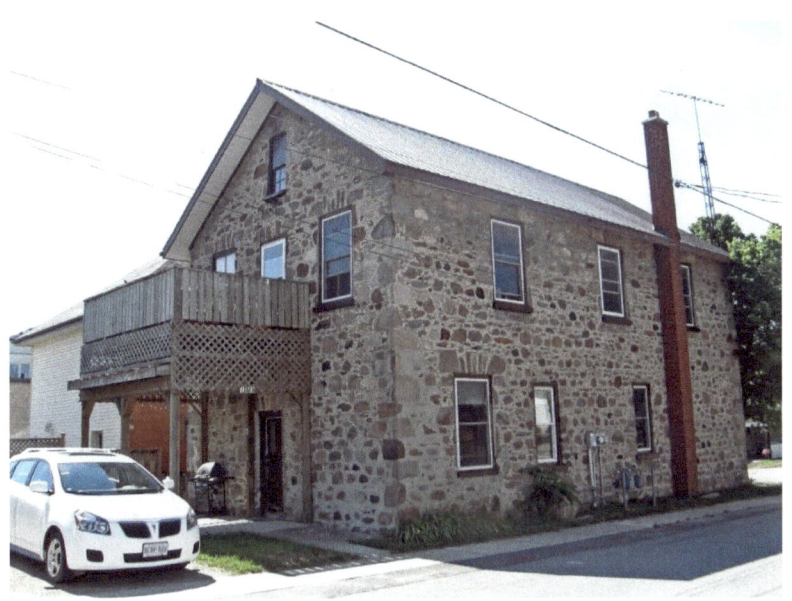

#183 – Gothic Revival - cobblestone architecture

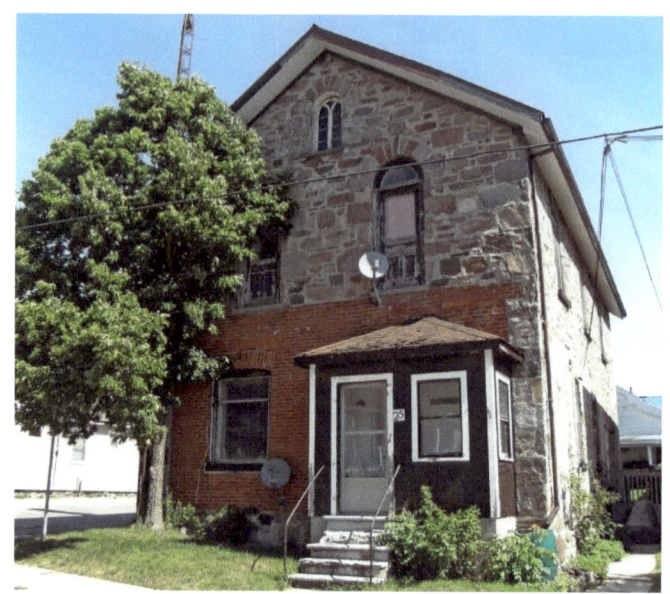

#25 - Cobblestone - Gothic

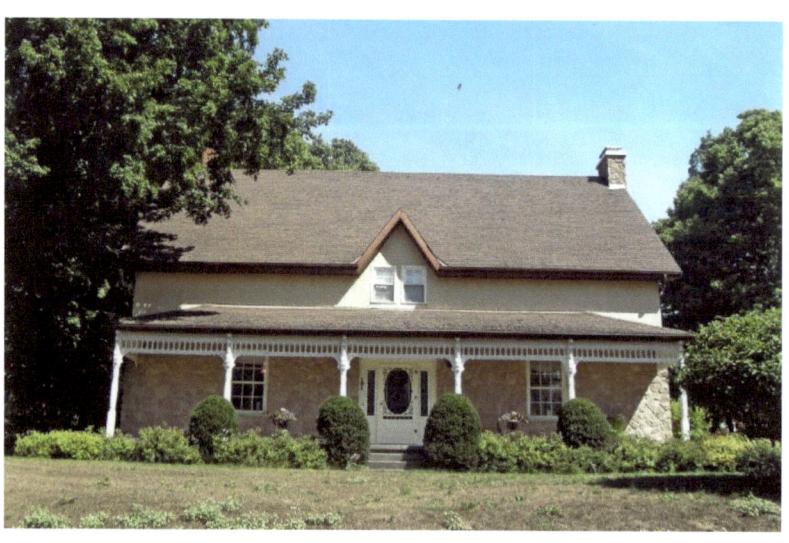

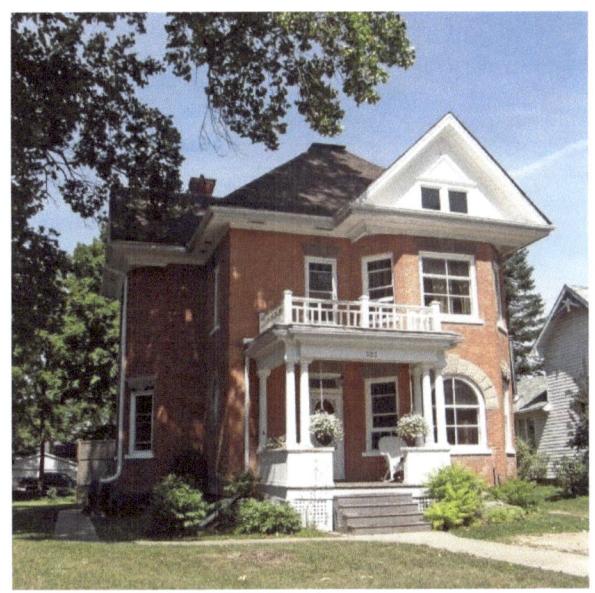

#332 - Edwardian – second floor balcony,
voussoirs and keystones

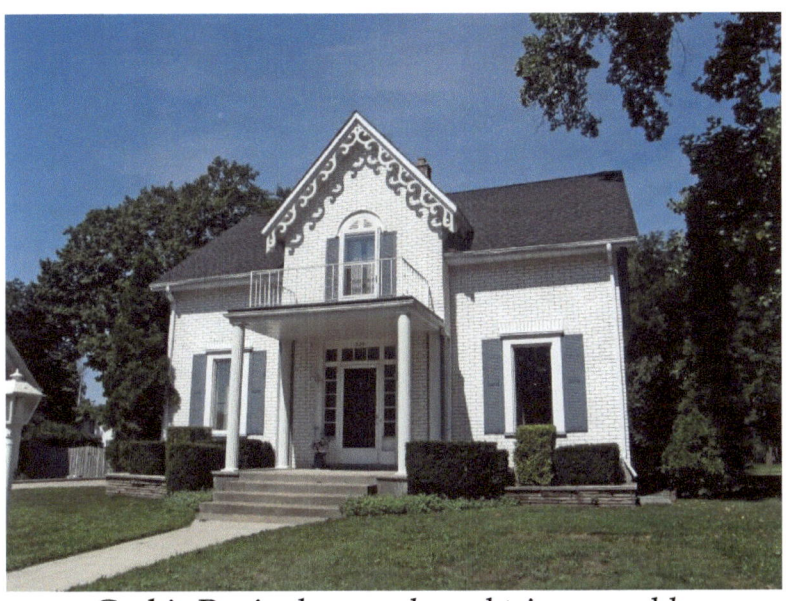

Gothic Revival, verge board trim on gable

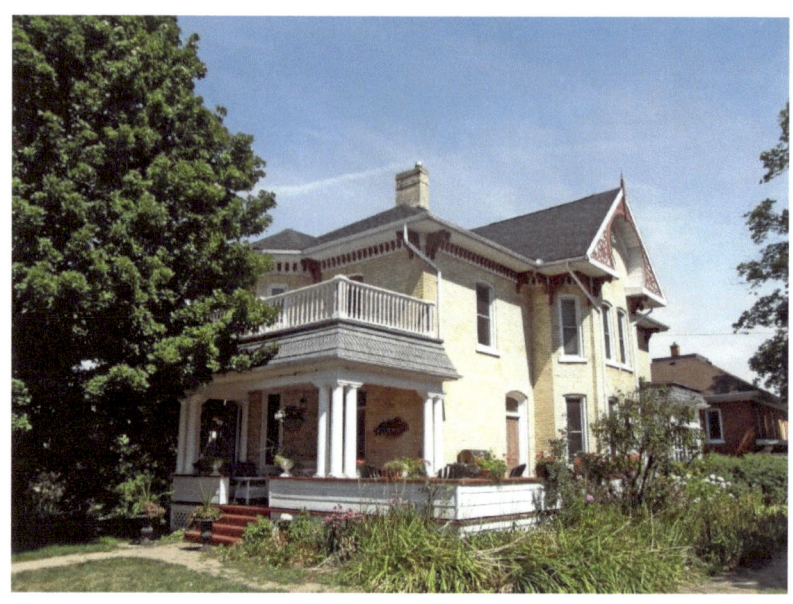

Two-and-a-half storey tower-like bay with verge board trim
on gable, second floor balcony

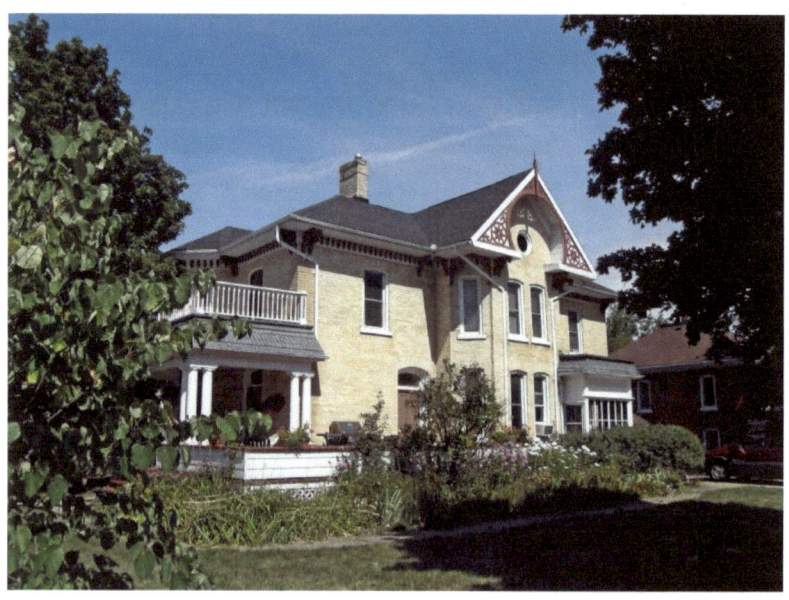

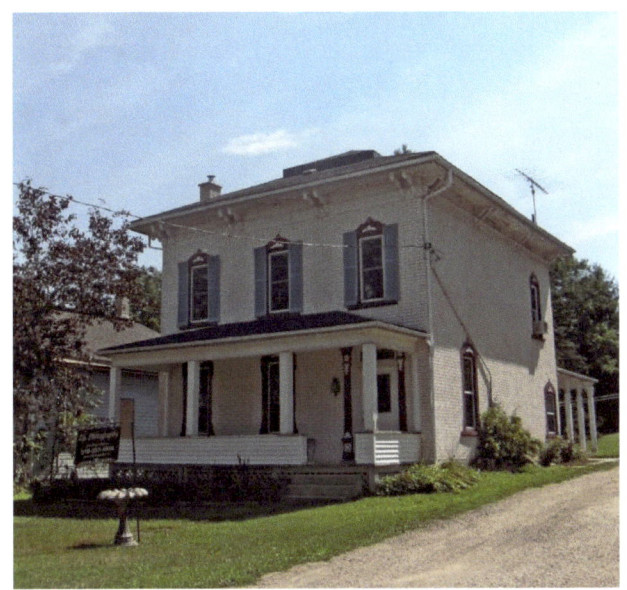

Italianate, cornice brackets, dentil moulding

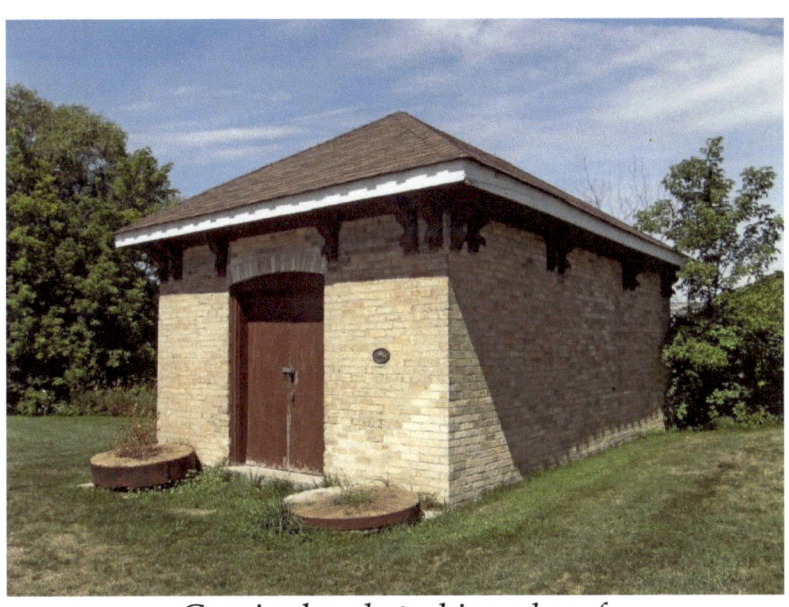

Cornice brackets, hipped roof

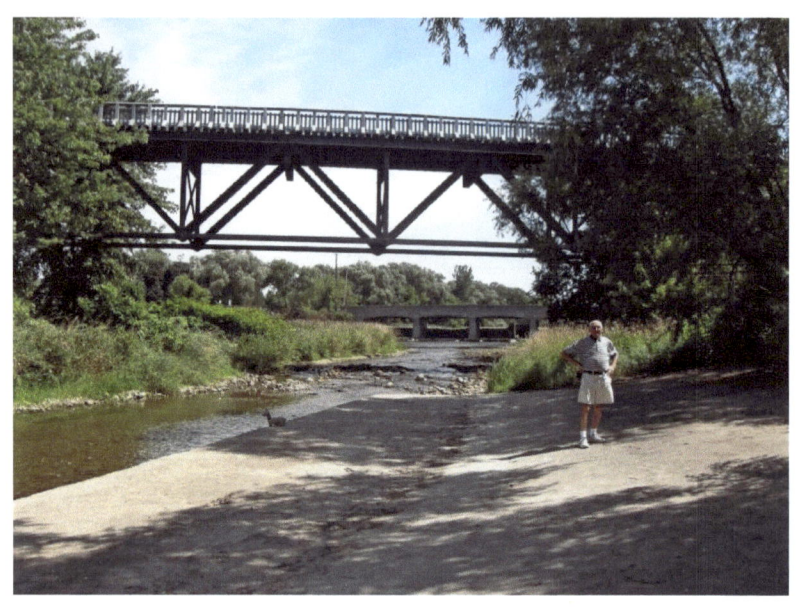

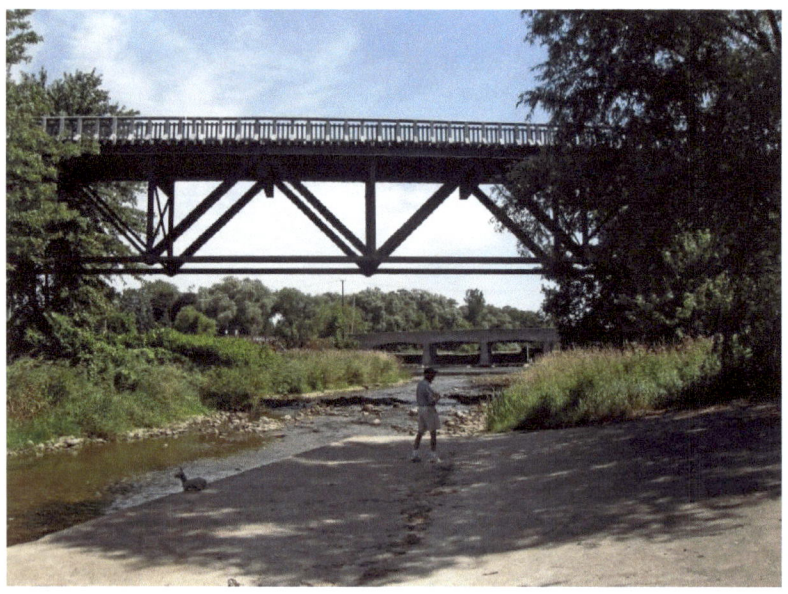

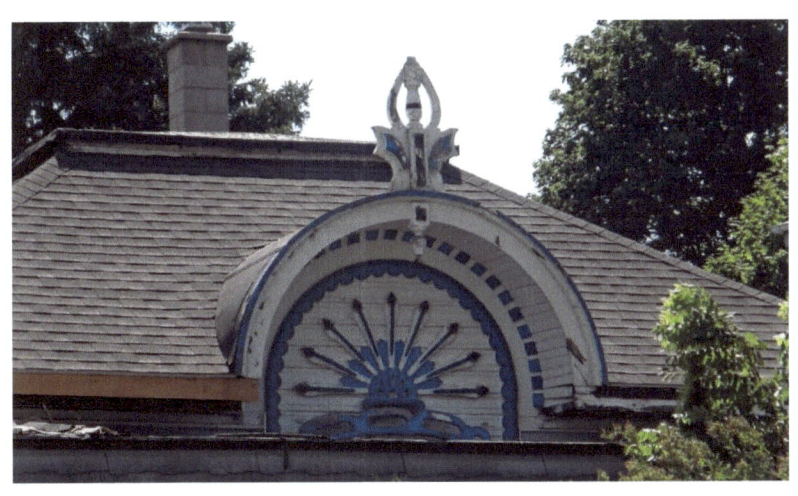

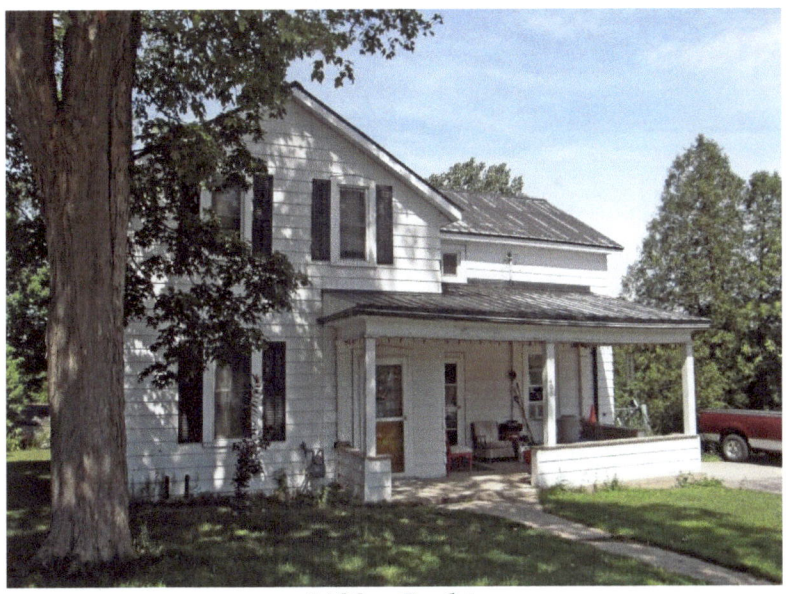

#408 - Gothic

Blyth

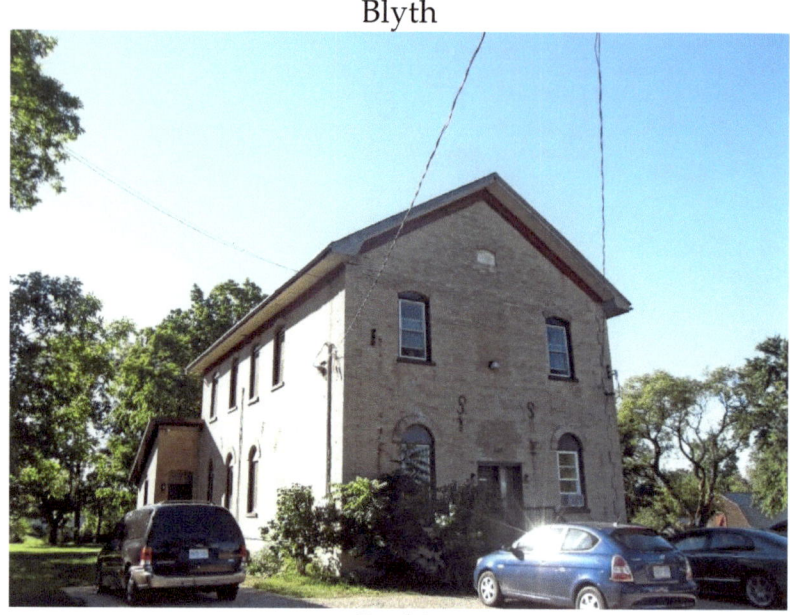

Gothic

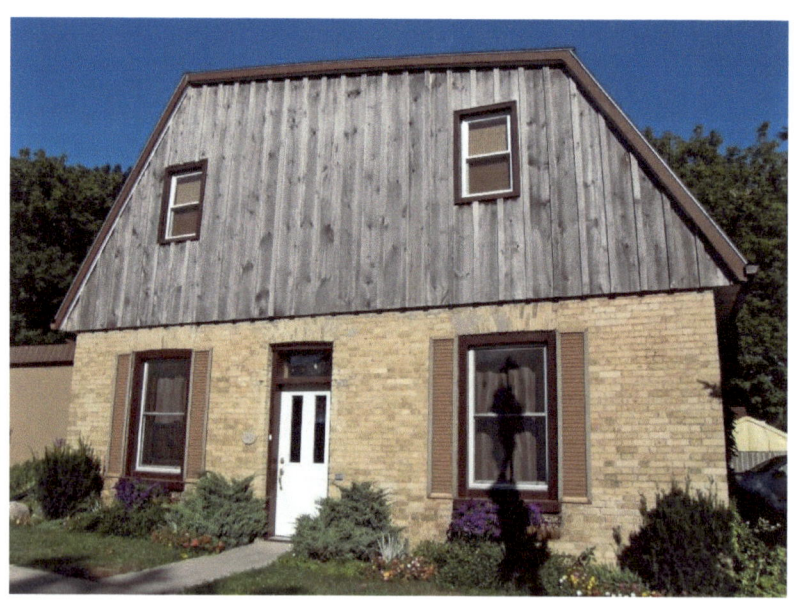

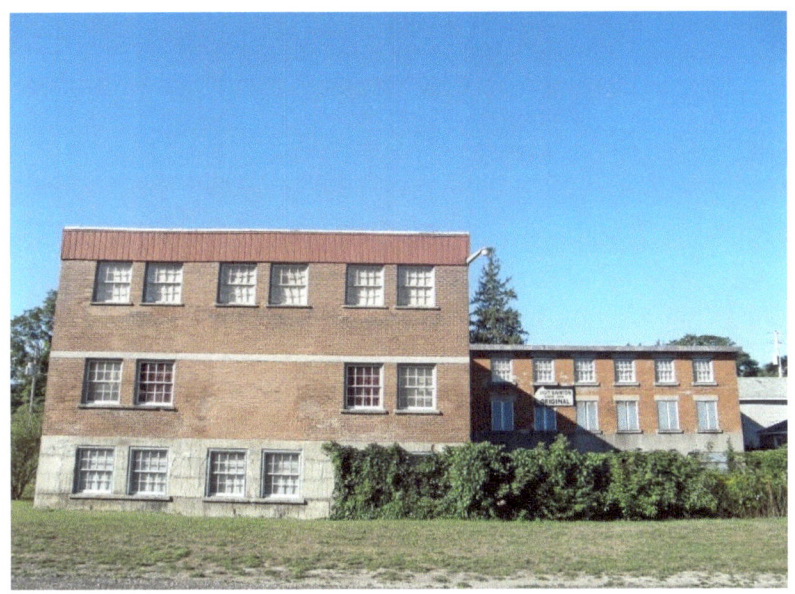

Bainton's Leather since 1894

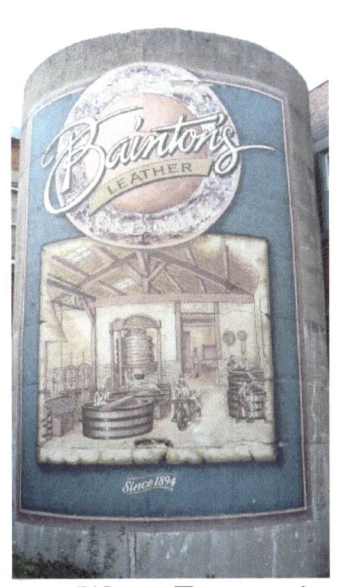

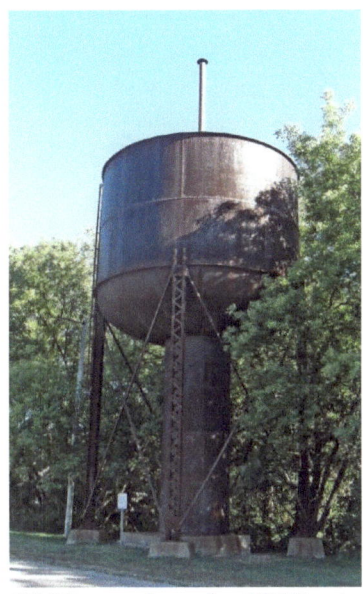

Water Tower – in the late 1800s and early 1900s, trains stopped at water towers like this to fill their reservoirs. The power generated by the seam drove the engines.

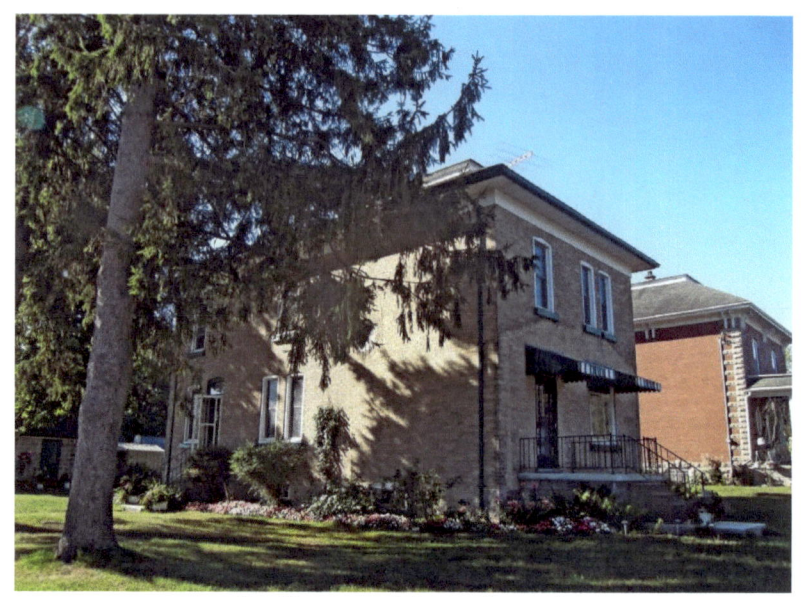

Italianate, hipped roof

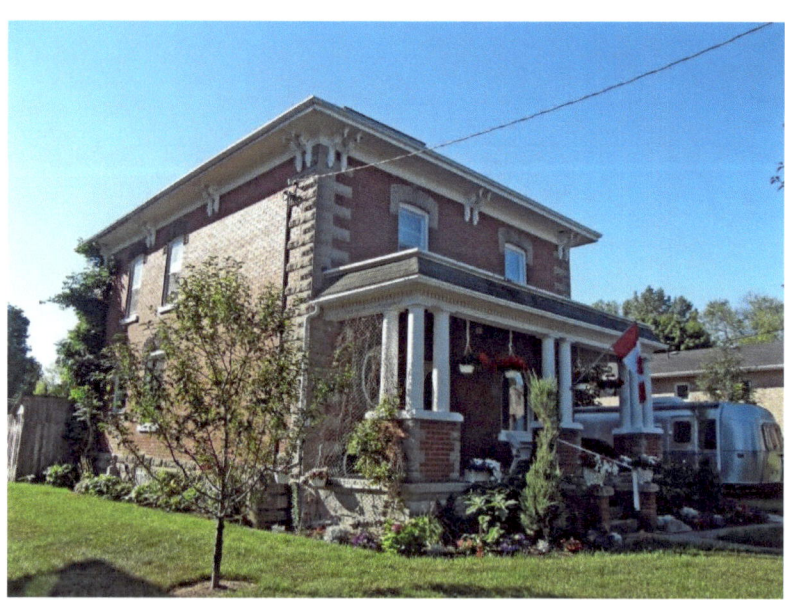

Italianate, hipped roof, cornice brackets, corner quoins

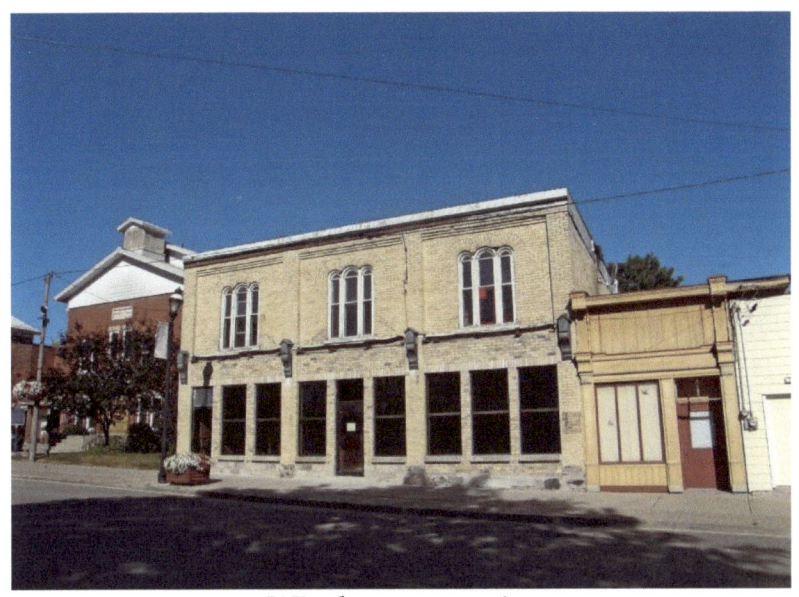

Window voussoirs

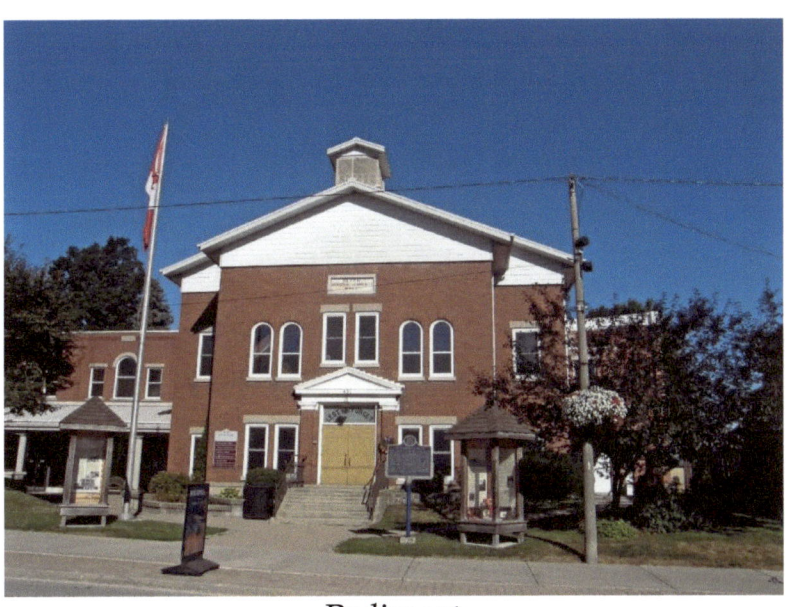

Pediment

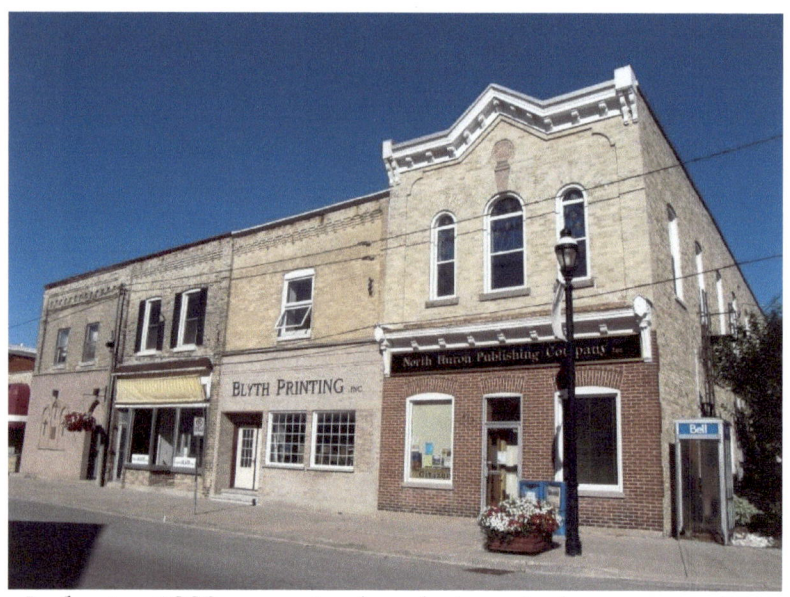

Industry 1888 - cornice brackets, window voussoirs, bevelled dentil moulding

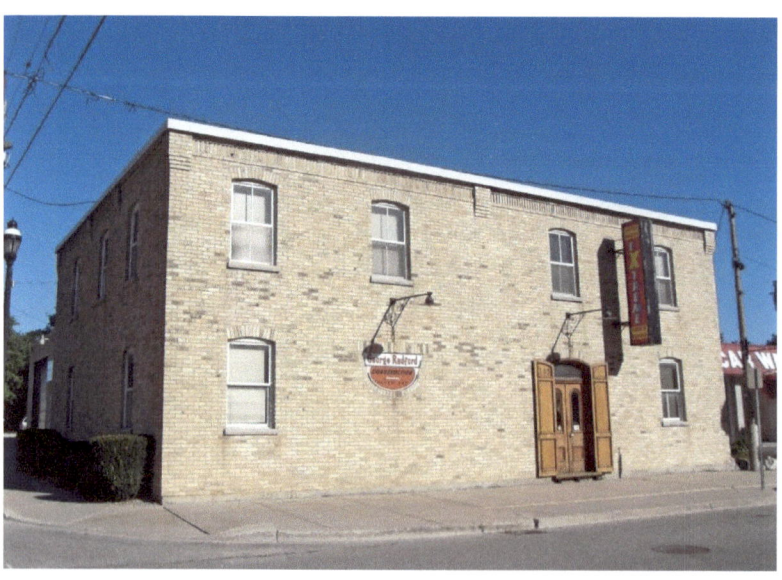

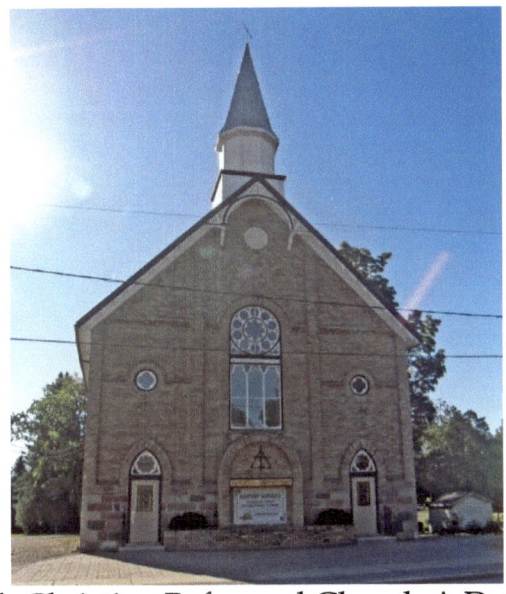

Blyth Christian Reformed Church A.D. 1889,
Gothic, rose window

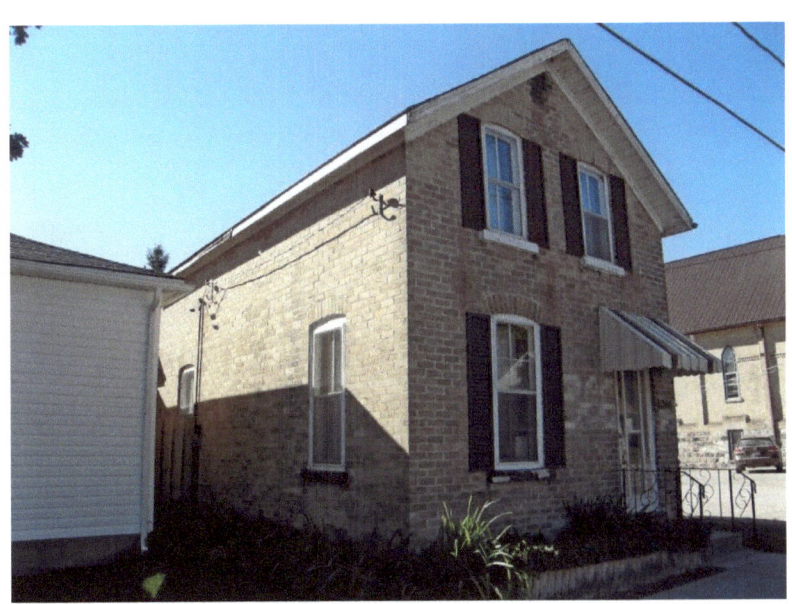

Gothic – yellow brick

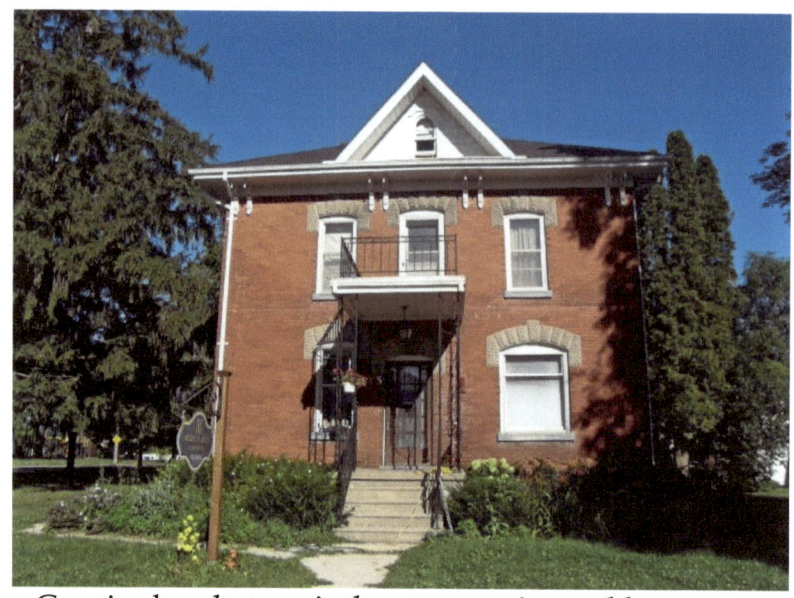

Cornice brackets, window voussoirs and keystones

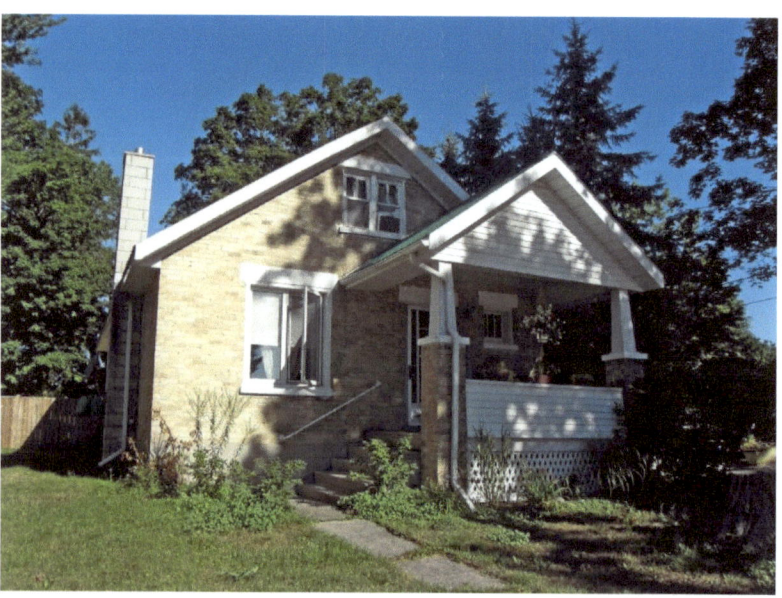

Cape Dutch style architecture

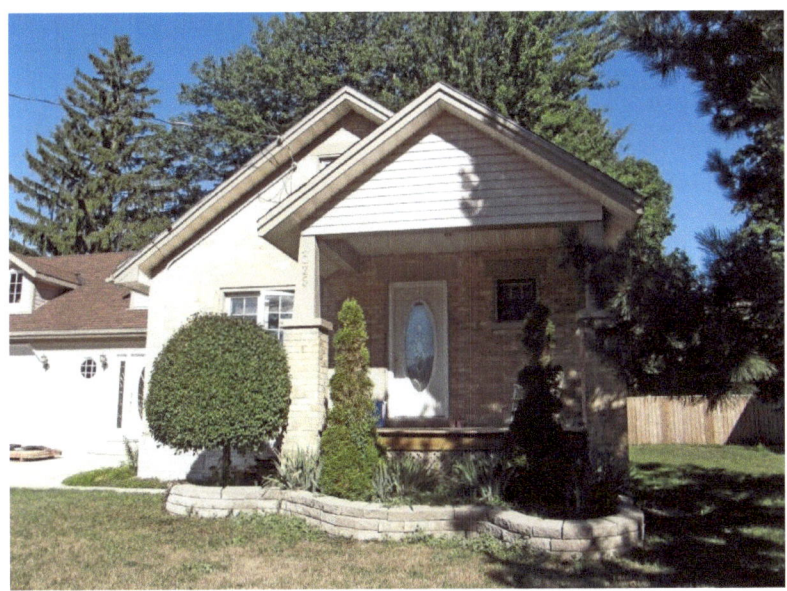

Cape Dutch style architecture

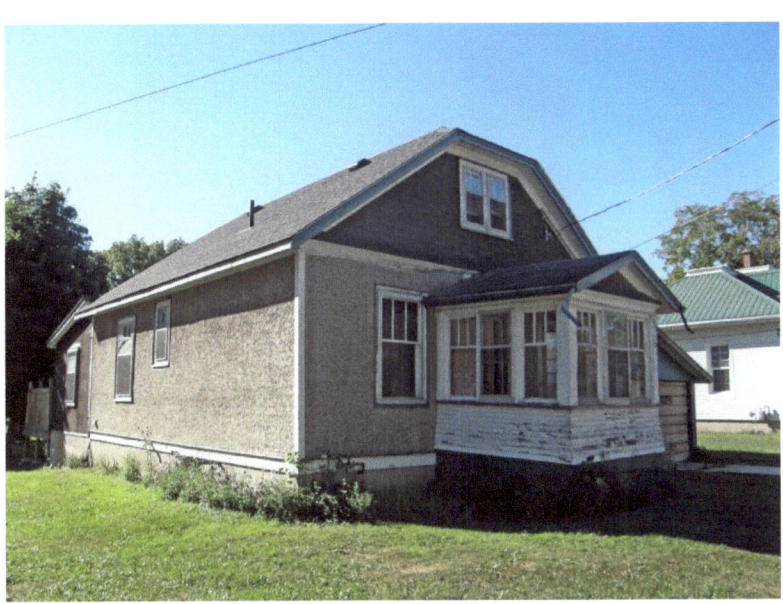

Cape Dutch style architecture

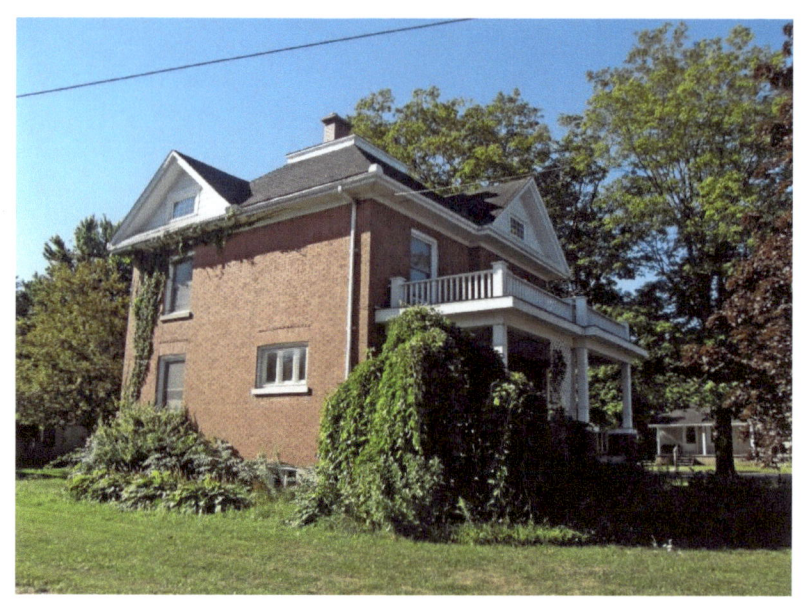

Edwardian – second floor balcony

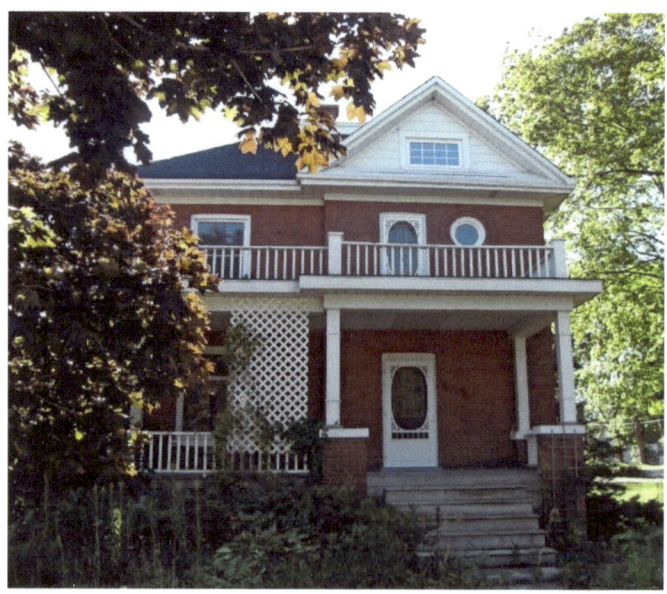

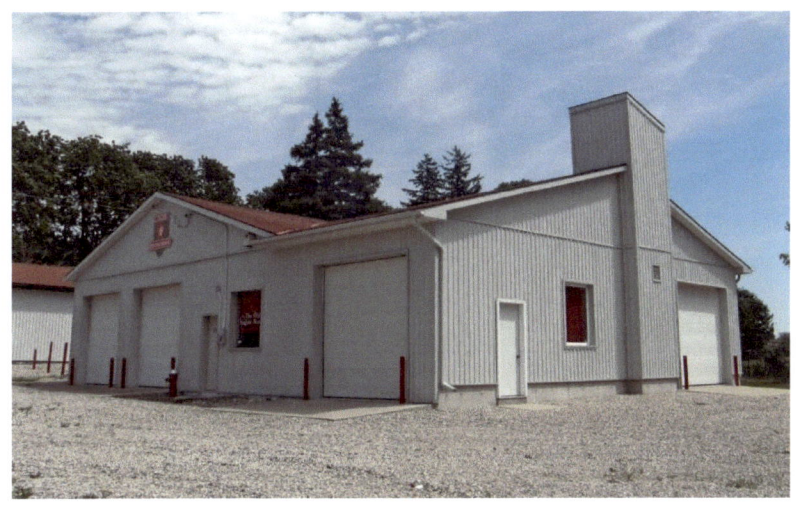

Engine House

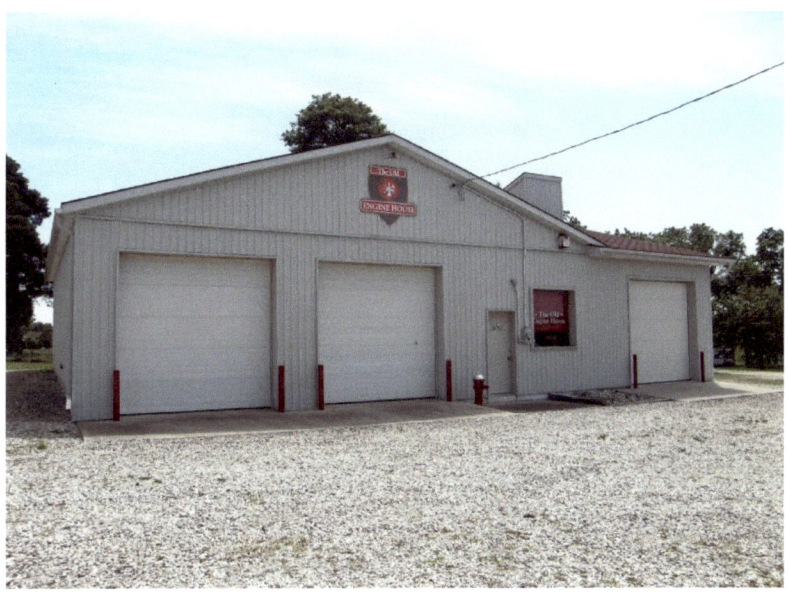

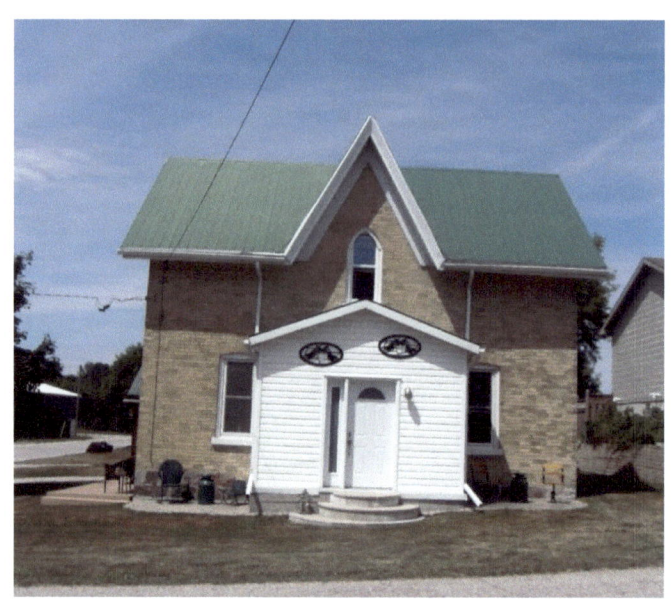

Gothic Revival

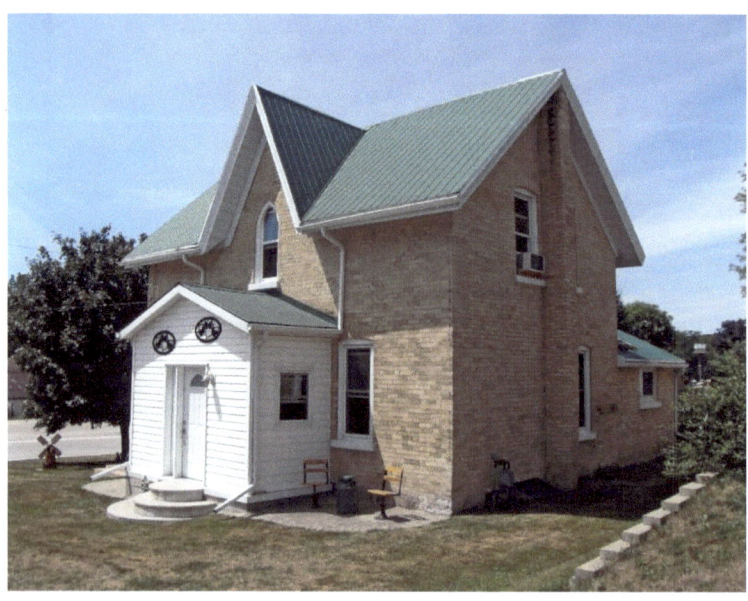

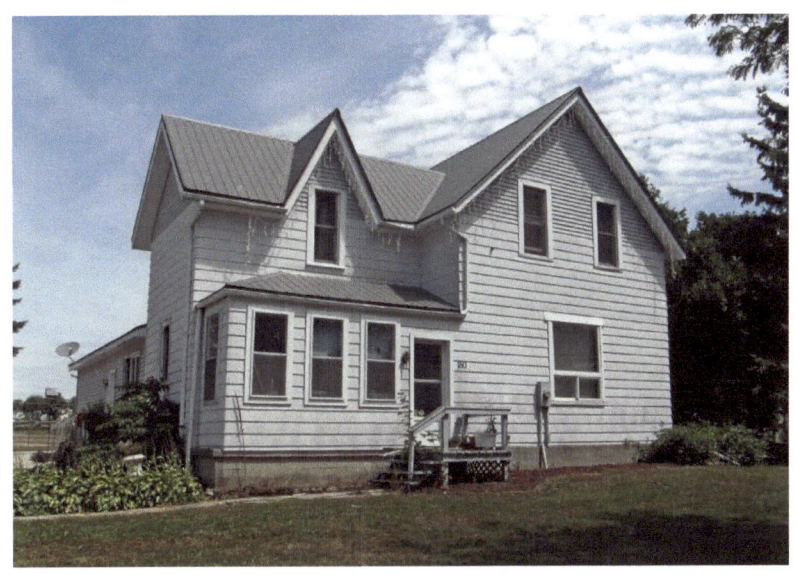

Gothic Revival

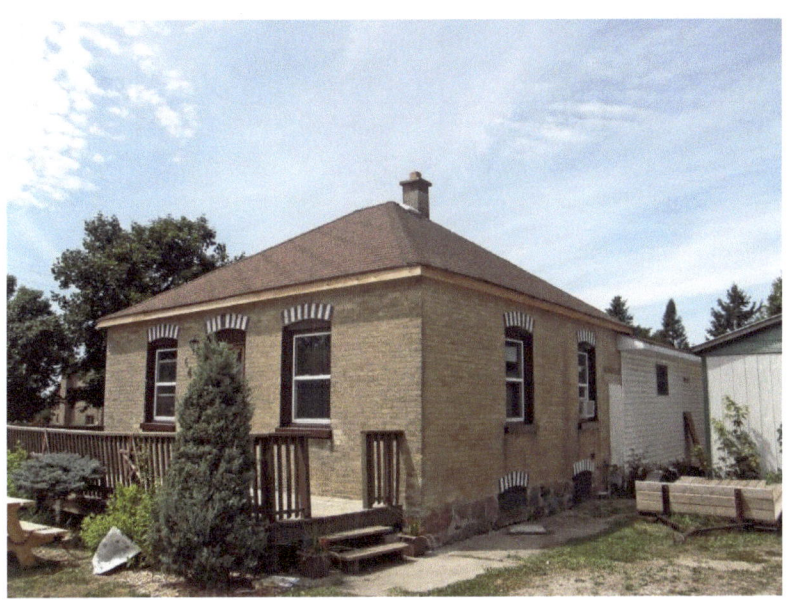

Hipped roof

Architectural Terms

Bay Window: A window that projects out from a wall, in a semicircular, rectangular, or polygonal design. Used frequently in Gothic and Victorian designs. Example: see Page 41	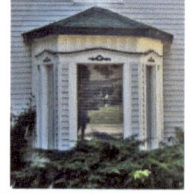
Brackets: a decorative or weight-bearing structural element which forms a right angle with one side against a wall and the other under a projecting surface such as an eave or roof. Example: see Page 19	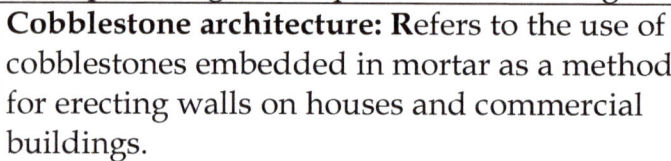
Buttress: a masonry structure built against or projecting from a wall which serves to support or reinforce the wall. In Canadian architecture, they are sometimes used for decoration. Example: Wingham Baptist Church, see Pg. 37	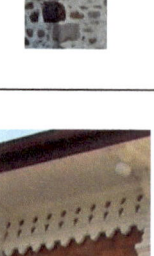
Cobblestone architecture: Refers to the use of cobblestones embedded in mortar as a method for erecting walls on houses and commercial buildings. Example: see Page 45	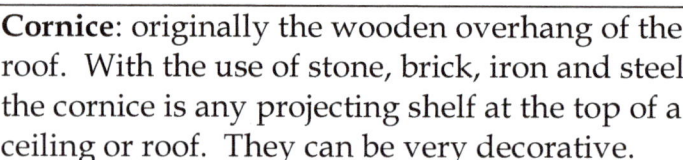
Cornice: originally the wooden overhang of the roof. With the use of stone, brick, iron and steel, the cornice is any projecting shelf at the top of a ceiling or roof. They can be very decorative. Example: see Page 41	

Cornice Return: decorative element on the end of a gable. Example: see Page 16	
Dentil Moulding: an even series of rectangles used as ornamental decoration in cornices. Example: see Page 7	
Dichromatic brickwork: the use of two colours of brick, tile or slate to decorate a façade. Example:	
Dormer: (French for "sleep") a gable end window that pierces through the plane of a sloping roof surface to create usable space in the top floor or attic of a building by adding headroom. Example: see Page 40	
Fretwork: interlaced decorative design resembling a bracket Example: see Page 15	
Gable: the triangular portion of a wall between the edges of a sloping roof. Example: see Page 42	
Hipped Roof: a roof where all sides slope downwards to the walls with no gables. Example: see Page 49	

Keystones and Voussoirs: a voussoir is a wedge-shaped element used in building an arch. A keystone is the central stone that locks all the stones into position, allowing the arch to bear weight. A keystone is often enlarged and embellished. Example:	
Lancet Window: a tall, narrow window with a pointed arch at its top. Example: Wingham Baptist church	
Mansard Roof: This style was popularized by Francois Mansart (1598-1666), an accomplished architect of the French Baroque period and especially fashionable during the Second French Empire (1852-1870). This roof is almost flat on the top section, with two slopes on each of its sides with the lower slope at a steeper angle than the upper and having dormer windows. Example: Town Hall, see Page 10	
Pediment: a triangular section above the horizontal structure (entablature), typically supported by columns. The inside of the triangle is called the tympanum. Example: Blyth, see Page 55	

Quoin: masonry blocks at the corner of a wall, often a decorative feature, usually larger or of a different colour than the rest of the wall. Example: see Page 35	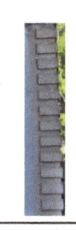
Rose Window: a circular window with ornamental tracery radiating from the centre. Example: Blyth Christian Reformed Church, see Page 57	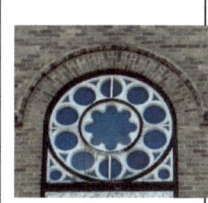
Turret: a small tower that projects from the wall of a building. Example:	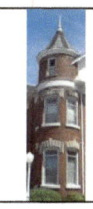
Vergeboard and Finial: also called bargeboards – hang from the projecting end of a roof and are often elaborately carved and ornamented. **Finial:** ornament added to the top of a gable, pinnacle, canopy or spire – a Gothic element.	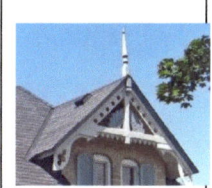

Beaux Arts: Promoters of this style sought to express the classical principles on a grand and imposing scale. Many of the Beaux Arts buildings were banks, post offices, and railway stations. The Ontario Beaux Arts style is eclectic mixing elements of Classical, Renaissance and Baroque. Often the designs have a temple-like façade, pedimented porticos, balustrades, capitals in many styles. Example: see Page 35	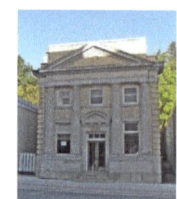
Cape Dutch architecture is a traditional Afrikaner architectural style found mostly in the Western Cape of South Africa. The initial settlers of the Cape were primarily Dutch. When the Dutch came to Ontario, they brought with them building concepts from their own native lands. Architecture from the 18th and early 19th centuries in Ontario includes a wide assortment of detailing and ornament all applied to a basic building design centred around the fireplace and the source of water. Example: Blyth – see Page 59	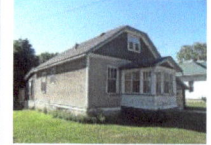

Edwardian, 1900-1930 – This style bridges the ornate and elaborate styles of the Victorian era and the simplified styles of the 20th century. Balanced facades, simple roof lines, dormer windows, large front porches, and smooth brick surfaces are its characteristics. Example: see Page 47	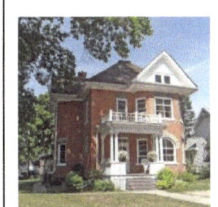
Gothic Revival, 1830-1890 – These decorative buildings have sharply-pitched gables with highly detailed verge boards, pointed-arch window openings, and dichromatic brickwork. It is a common style in Ontario. Example: see Page 42	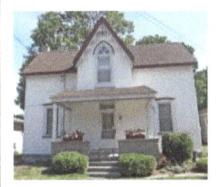
Italianate, 1850-1900 – It has wide-bracketed eaves, belvederes, wrap-around verandahs. Example: see Page 16	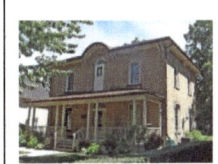
Queen Anne, 1885-1900 – This style is distinguished by an irregular outline featuring a combination of an offset tower, broad gables, projecting two-storey bays, verandahs, multi-sloped roofs, and tall, decorative chimneys. A mixture of brick and wood is common. Windows often have one large single-paned bottom sash and small panes in the upper sash. Example:	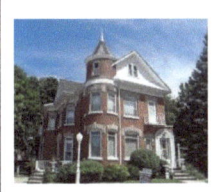
Second Empire, 1860-1880 – The mansard roof is the most noteworthy feature of this style and is evidence of the French origins. Projecting central towers and one or two-storey bays can also be present. Example:	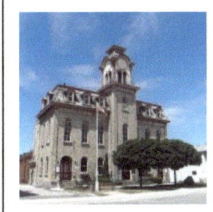

www.ingramcontent.com/pod-product-compliance
Lightning Source LLC
Chambersburg PA
CBHW040841180526
45159CB00001B/267